PENGUIN BOOKS
George III

Jeremy Black MBE is Emeritus Professor of History at Exeter University, Senior Fellow at Policy Exchange and Senior Fellow at the Center for the Study of America and the West at the Foreign Policy Research Institute in Philadelphia. His two major fields of scholarship are military history and eighteenth-century British history. Recent books include *War and Technology*, *Rethinking World War Two* and *England in the Age of Shakespeare*. He has held visiting chairs at a number of American institutions, including West Point, and received the Samuel Eliot Morison Prize from the Society for Military History in 2008.

T0004471

JEREMY BLACK

George III

Majesty and Madness

PENGUIN BOOKS

PENGUIN BOOKS

UK | USA | Canada | Ireland | Australia
India | New Zealand | South Africa

Penguin Books is part of the Penguin Random House group of companies
whose addresses can be found at global.penguinrandomhouse.com

First published by Allen Lane 2020
Published in Penguin Books 2023
001

Copyright © Jeremy Black, 2020

The moral right of the author has been asserted

Typeset by Jouve (UK), Milton Keynes
Printed and bound in Great Britain by Clays Ltd, Elcograf S.p.A.

The authorized representative in the EEA is Penguin Random House Ireland,
Morrison Chambers, 32 Nassau Street, Dublin DO2 YH68

A CIP catalogue record for this book is available from the British Library

ISBN: 978-0-141-99342-3

www.greenpenguin.co.uk

Penguin Random House is committed to a
sustainable future for our business, our readers
and our planet. This book is made from Forest
Stewardship Council® certified paper.

Contents

For John Cartafalsa and Lydia Dufour

George III and his family

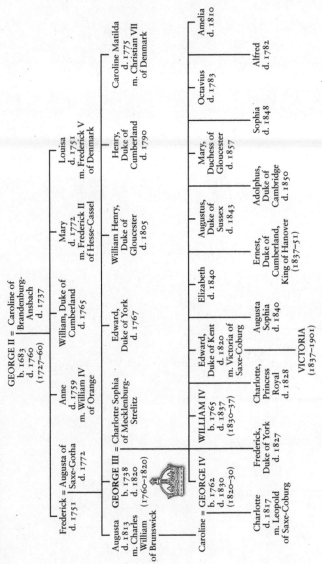

Preface

A focus during his lifetime both of hatred and of loyalty, George III is now best known for two reasons: his unsuccessful role in preventing American independence and his 'madness'. The former is endlessly refreshed by the American public and has been dramatically presented anew in the successful musical *Hamilton* (2015). The 'madness' is the basis for Alan Bennett's play *The Madness of George III* (1991), then his film *The Madness of King George* (1994). Each is important in constructing the prevalent image of the king, but, from his lifetime on, he was the subject of such image-making. It sat in an uneasy counterpoint to his life, which is our major topic.

I would like to thank Stuart Proffitt for inviting me to revisit George for this superb series. In 2006, I published a work of over 200,000 words dripping with footnotes. The chance to rethink the king and his importance, not least in the light of later work, is valuable, and the tautness of the length has helped me to focus on issues of crucial significance. I have benefited from opportunities to speak at the Guildhall in London, Mary Washington University, the University of Virginia, the American Museum in Bath and the Athenaeum.

I would like to thank Nigel Aston, Bruce Coleman, Grayson Ditchfield, Mike Duffy, Bill Gibson, Will Hay, Peter

PREFACE

Onuf, Jim Sack, Christopher Wright and Neil York for
commenting on an earlier draft. They are not responsible
for any errors. I have benefited greatly from the editorial
advice and the support of Stuart Proffitt. It is a great pleasure to dedicate this book to Colonel John B. Cartafalsa,
US Army, and his wife Lydia, and in so doing to note many
years of friendship and my appreciation for their welcom-
ing hospitality in New York, a city that toppled its statue of
George in 1776.

George III

I
An Earnest Young Man

Becoming king at the age of twenty-two in 1760, George was the youngest in that position since Edward VI, a child, in 1547, and there has been no equivalent since. It is all too easy to forget his youth, but it was very important to the determined way in which he took up the charge. So also were two other factors: the education he had received, and his reaction against his elderly predecessor, his grandfather George II (1683–1760, r. 1727–60).

Born amid the grandeur of Norfolk House, St James's Square, London, on 24 May (old style; 4 June new style) 1738, the future George III was the first son, and second child, of Frederick, Prince of Wales and his young wife, Augusta of Saxe-Gotha. His names, George William Frederick, proclaimed his impeccable dynastic and Whig credentials. However, such names were no security for a child born two months premature, and there were doubts that the prince would survive, but Mary Smith, one of the key figures who so easily slip from attention, proved an effective wet-nurse. Characteristically, George, who had the true charm of generosity of spirit, not the false charm of glib ease, showed gratitude. He appointed Mary his laundress after he became

king, and when she died he had her youngest daughter succeed her.

At the age of four, the prince was described as a lovely
child and as fat,[1] at that time a sign of health. With early
years being in some respects more private than for a modern
prince, one of the first accounts is of his acting, aged ten, the
role of the virtuous hero in a children's production of Joseph
Addison's famous play *Cato* (1713), albeit with a new pro-
logue to speak: 'What, tho' a boy! It may with truth be said,
/ A boy in England born, in England bred.' Republican virtue,
not imperial monarchy, was a theme of this Whig text which
George Washington liked and had staged for his officers at
Valley Forge. Another Whig classic, Nicholas Rowe's *Lady
Jane Grey* (1715), an account of exemplary Protestant virtue
set in English history, was also staged by Frederick's children.

George's first letter, a formal one of 1749 sent to his grandfather, the king, acknowledged the honour done by awarding
him the Order of the Garter.[2] The following year, George
visited Oakley House in Buckinghamshire with his father,
but little is known of their relationship. In late 1749, Frederick
set up a timetable for George and his brother Edward, later
Duke of York. Lessons took up the morning and late afternoon, with a play hour and the main meal in the early
afternoon. Little time was set aside for outdoor recreations.

For some years the young man sought to follow the political beliefs of his father. These focused on the idea of
a 'Patriot King', a monarch who could rise above party
interests, and, notably, the commitment of George I and
George II to the governing Whigs. Based on the arguments
of Henry, Viscount Bolingbroke, who had, from the 1720s,

sought to articulate a 'Country' opposition to the governing Whigs, this idea focused assumptions about the proper character of kingship. In particular, the 'Patriot King' was seen as a national redeemer, a figure who could mitigate what Tory and opposition Whig critics saw as the unfortunate impact of the Whig monopoly of power that had followed the Hanoverian succession in 1714, especially on British political culture.

As an aspect of his education in constitutionalism, the young prince earnestly developed these precepts in a number of memoranda. He was to be thrust to the fore because his father predeceased him on 20 March 1751, a key episode in George's personal as well as political life. Frederick's unexpected death meant that George would not face the opportunities and problems of coming to the throne much later in life. Also there would be no earlier experience under a Frederick I in bedding down the concept of a 'Patriot King'.

The difficult George II did not extend to his daughter-in-law or his grandchildren the loathing he had shown for his troublesome eldest son, who had proved only too willing to align with opposition politicians. Augusta, who survived till 1772, sought the king's protection for herself and her children, and he extended it, going to see her, and urging George and Edward to be brave. The young George succeeded at once to his father's title of Duke of Edinburgh, and he was created Prince of Wales and Earl of Chester that April. Nevertheless, the prince did not receive a separate household until 1756, and relations between Augusta and George II deteriorated over financial provision. The prince was clearly affected by his mother's anger, which indeed contributed to the feeling of lost rights and misuse of power that shaped his attitude to the political system. Meanwhile, the sense of the prince as a political property was seen in 1752–3 when Simon, 1st Earl Harcourt, who had become his governor in 1751, backed by Thomas Hayter, Bishop of Norwich, the preceptor charged with the oversight of his education, claimed that Harcourt's deputy Andrew Stone was a quasi-Jacobite pushing unwelcome Tory views, charges that Stone held off but that affected the image of the young George.

A related aspect of George's upbringing and his determination to improve the country was provided by his strong religious commitment. Again, there was a contrast to his two predecessors and, instead, a return to the piety and devotion of Queen Anne (r. 1702–14). This commitment is apt to be downplayed in a secular age, but it was fundamental to George's life, character and policies, and contemporaries noted the energy with which he said his amens. This was a matter not only of zeal but also of alignment. George I and George II might have been Supreme Governors of the Church of England and in communion with the Church, dutifully attending Anglican worship, but they were Lutherans by upbringing and practice. Although not especially devout, they were observant and both insisted on choosing their chaplains rather than allowing them to become ministerial appointments. An Anglican from the outset, George III also took his piety into his politics, with the idea of service and commitment being important to both; but this drive meant that George found it difficult to understand, let alone sympathize with, those who held different views or followed other lifestyles.

The early influences on George contributed to guiding his sense of seriousness in an explicitly religious direction, and to ensuring that his Christian convictions were very much framed in terms of duty. Lutheran by upbringing, his mother Augusta became a devout Anglican, particularly critical of latitudinarianism, and she had a strong influence on George. Clerics, successively Francis Ayscough, Thomas Hayter and John Thomas, were prominent in his upbringing; and Hayter, a firm opponent of popery and licentiousness, placed a very strong emphasis on Divine Providence in his sermons. Moreover, John Stuart, 3rd Earl of Bute, his adviser and confidant from 1755, was a Scottish Episcopalian, convinced of the importance of Christian teaching in royal education.

A sense of struggle played a role in his self-identity and shaped his assessment of other people. Those who struggled to command themselves and prevail over temptation earned his respect, while others who surrendered he distrusted.

In November 1759, when he was twenty-one, George fell in love with Lady Sarah Lennox, a beautiful fifteen-year-old who was the sister of Charles, 3rd Duke of Richmond and sister-in-law of Henry Fox. George, however, realized that this was unlikely to be an acceptable match, both because she was a commoner and because Fox was a highly controversial politician. He accepted Bute's advice not to pursue the matter, but, despite his belief that only marriage would end the struggle between prudence and his desire for women, was unwilling, while still a prince, to seek a German princess, which reflected his view that any such negotiation would give too much opportunity to George II to meddle in his affairs. Indeed, in 1755, Augusta and Prince George thwarted the king when he tried to arrange a marriage between the prince and Sophie Caroline of Brunswick-Wolfenbüttel, a proposal that reflected the king's wish to improve relations with Prussia.

According to Fox, at his first birthday ball as king, George only had eyes for Lady Sarah: 'He stopped very remarkably as he was going and turned and spoke again and again as if he could not force himself from her.'[3] In 1788, while very ill, George raved about Lady Sarah, which contributed to the depiction of him as a highly sexual puritan suffering from repressed sexuality, a depiction that may have had some truth in 1759,[4] but that is based on an inaccurately negative portrayal of his marriage. There is no sound basis for the reports that George in 1759 had a relationship with, indeed secretly married, the 'very engaging' Hannah Lightfoot, a Quaker by whom he was supposed to have had a son, George Rex, and who was married off in return for a large sum.

George thought it necessary that, once he became king, he should take a central political role, which he saw not only as his constitutional responsibility but also as his moral duty. Particularly as a young man, this moral sense helped characterize George as a prig who regretted the lack of piety and virtue among others, a view he expressed to Bute.[5] George's self-righteousness, which owed much to his mother's emphasis on piety and virtue, gave particular energy to the drive for change usually associated with the heir. Indeed, in many respects George assumed middle-aged attitudes when young, in modern terms a 'fogey' Prince of

Wales, and remained true to them for the rest of his life, always wishing to project a respectable image, and having more scope to do so the older he became. Shortly after George's accession, a retired senior official observed:

> The character given me of our present sovereign by an authentic hand not to be suspected of flattery is that he has naturally a most deep and lively sense of true religion and every social virtue; is master of his passions and appetites, and can without pain sacrifice any private inclination of his own to the public good; is perfectly instructed in our constitution, and resolved to act conformably to it, and as far as in him lies to preserve the union he found subsisting among his subjects ... Several particulars I have heard that indicate much affability and good nature.[6]

Conscientiousness might seem the obvious definition of George's character, but his sense of duty was motivated by a commitment that deserves more attention. At any rate, he regarded himself, and was seen, as indolent in his early years, probably due to the difficulty of his circumstances after the death of his father; but, under Bute's careful political tutelage, he came to work much harder and to have a stronger sense of responsibility. Indeed, this led him to lament misspent time and to promise improvement.[7]

As a prince, George's lifestyle was certainly very different from those of his two predecessors, who were brought up to the saddle of command as well as that of hunting, for as young members of a German princely house they were expected to fight. Their lifetime was also that of a style of monarchy that might be described as baroque, in that the current influence, radiating from Louis XIV's palace of Versailles, was a new version of the traditional royal emphasis on show and splendour. This was certainly not the monarch as servant of the people, let alone the quasi-bureaucrat seen with the 'Enlightened Despots' of the late eighteenth century, and for neither George I nor George II is there much surviving in terms of correspondence.

George III personified a very different style of monarchy. For him, diligence was at once public and private, secular and ecclesiastical. Augusta and Bute were the key influences on him as he grew to manhood, and Augusta's success in keeping him away from louche aristocratic influence, together with her piety, helped mould George's character and give him the taste for a somewhat isolated domesticity which he subsequently reproduced in his own family. Taking charge of George's education in 1755, Bute was Augusta's key adviser, rather than, as was widely alleged, her lover. He came to play the same role for George, serving as a surrogate father. A wealthy and well-connected aristocrat, but not close to the Whig oligarchs, Bute tried to pass on his well-developed artistic, cultural and scientific interests. However, George's confidence in this quasi-paternal figure provided a basis for the charges of undue favouritism and manipulation by Bute that were to colour George's reputation after he came to the throne. George's letters to Bute, whom he called from 1757 'My Dearest Friend', reveal a sense of dependence, as well as frustration that his education had been neglected. George's promises of personal reformation in order to make himself suited to his role indicate the degree to which he saw his kingship as a mission and a self-improvement project.

As king, George III's timetable and correspondence denoted effort. That effort was not predominantly military, and one of the most significant contrasts between George and his predecessors was his lack of military experience. If he was not unique in this respect, as Louis XVI also had none, he was highly unusual: contemporaries not noted for their military activity, such as Louis XV, had been on campaign, as had every English male monarch over the past quarter-millennium, bar Edward VI and James I. This was not for want of effort on George's part, as he wished to serve in the Seven Years War (1756–63), only to be thwarted by his grandfather, who had led an army into battle at Dettingen in 1743. When George III had an opportunity to serve in 1761–2, he did not do so: command in Germany would not have matched his political priorities and etiquette, and practicality precluded command in Portugal in 1762. George, however, like other non-combatant monarchs, did adopt military poses when he later reviewed troops and warships. It was more convenient to review troops in the London area, and he did so with some frequency. Frederick, Duke of York, who became his favourite son, was a martial figure.

Instead of a military life, the young prince was given a wide-ranging and thorough education. Reflecting the cultural interests of both his parents, George applied himself to the study of music, architecture and drawing, and developed a discriminating eye for paintings. Augusta was a patron of the architect William Chambers, who had a significant artistic influence on George, teaching him architectural drawing three mornings a week and also providing him with guidance to the new archaeological discoveries, not least Robert Wood's work on Baalbec and Palmyra. George was to produce a large number of architectural drawings. He was also taught perspectival drawing by Joshua Kirby, who, like Chambers, was to enjoy his patronage when king, while his surviving landscape drawings include many classical buildings. George also learned languages, read history and became used to writing at length. He was a much more industrious pupil than his sons were to be.

George II, however, kept the young prince away from political responsibility or governmental experience. In part, this treatment (which ironically reflected that under which the king himself had suffered when he was Prince of Wales) reflected the carry-over from his strong hostility to Frederick, in part a determination to retain the power of kingship, which, once divided with an heir, was much less than the sum of the parts, and in part a hostility to those who looked politically to the prince, notably opposition Whigs. As the theme of a Patriot King was used against George II, it was not surprising that the king resented the prince's 'patriotic' pretensions, and neither behaved in a particularly attractive light. Keeping Bute from power exacerbated Prince George's alienation and contributed to the degree to which a change in measures was expected by, and from, the younger George when he became king.

The nearest parallels for succession at an early age were not encouraging. Among monarchs who came to the throne young, Frederick II of Prussia (1712–86, r. 1740–86) was a success, but the vigour of Joseph II of Austria (1741–90, r. 1780–90; emperor from 1765) was not matched by prudence. Peter III, who came to the throne of Russia in 1762 aged thirty-four, was far more foolish than Joseph, being murdered in a coup staged on behalf of his wife and successor, Catherine II, within a year. Also succeeding his grandfather, Louis XVI came to the throne of France in 1774 at nineteen fired up with ideals, notably to shake up the political situation. He wanted to reverse his grandfather's contentious policies and to stand forth as a king who embodied a fresh start through a qualified restoration of the earlier constitutional position. Fifteen years later, France was in crisis.

George II died on 25 October 1760 at Kensington Palace. Having risen early, as was his habit, and drunk his chocolate, he retired to relieve himself on his close-stool, where, alone, he died from a heart attack at 7.30 a.m. His valet, Schröder, heard a noise and found George dead on the floor.

Time would tell whether the ongoing war abroad, and the new political confidence and co-operation that it had helped create at home, would bring further benefits to the new king. George III was an unknown quantity when he came to the throne. From his period as prince, he brought a potent mix of determination, commitment and self-righteousness. This was a difficult mix, for himself and others, as was his combination of self-confidence and self-doubt.

2

A Young King

> Born and educated in this country I glory in the name of
> Britain; and the peculiar happiness of my life will ever con-
> sist in promoting the welfare of a people whose loyalty and
> warm affection to me I consider as the great and most per-
> manent security of my throne.[1]

George's addition to the draft for his first speech from the
throne, delivered on 18 November 1760, was part of the
continuance after his accession on 25 October of Patriot
gestures and, notably, of differentiating himself from Hanover; but, aside from his striking of such notes, George's
personality and youth contributed to his positive reputation, Henry Fox noting of his first week as king that he
received 'in the most gracious and pleasing manner crowds
of people without number (and by the way the King acts
his part in public well)'.[2] For George, patriotism came with
piety, both linked to a sense of duty, and Thomas Secker,
Archbishop of Canterbury, recorded of the coronation in
1761 that he stood at Westminster Abbey 'on the right hand
of the King, who was very attentive to the delivery of the
regalia, and rectified several mistakes of the Heralds with
much good humour'. During the service, 'In reading the

Declaration to the King, I omitted in one place the word *profess*; but he spoke it, giving me a smiling look.'[3]

Patterns that emerge in hindsight can be misleading, not least because they privilege the perspective of posterity over the experience of contemporaries. Yet, there was a pattern for George that is instructive in that it leads to the lesson of hard-won experience. A young man with expectations of change becomes a young king in a hurry to transform the situation. Even the poorly organized coronation suggested room for improvement: the mislaying of the sword of state led to a delay of three hours, and the banquet was chaotic, with no places for some of the leading aristocrats, while the champion's horse backed into the new king, who lost his temper and berated the acting earl marshal after the ceremony. Something of a perfectionist, George found reality, in the shape of the critical and/or unwilling responses of others, as well as his own limitations, repeatedly galling in the 1760s, but he learned to cope and play a major role in creating a new ministerial pattern that brought stability in the early 1770s. Reality, in the same shape, then brought an unexpected total breakdown in America in 1775 and, eventually, a near political collapse in Britain in 1782-4. There was again a fresh start through a new ministerial system which had both the strength to bring stability in the peace years that ended in 1793, and the resilience thereafter that proved crucial in the face of repeated failures and problems in dealing with revolutionary pressures, internal and external.

For George, there was pleasure in each of these periods of success, but much anger and some soul-searching in those of failure. Anger and soul-searching were more apparent in the 1760s. 'Dropping the Pilot', the famous 1890 Tenniel caricature in *Punch* of the young Emperor Wilhelm II of Germany dispensing with the long-standing chancellor, Otto von Bismarck, might also seem appropriate to George's parting with the two principal figures of the politics of the mid to late 1750s and of the wartime ministry, William Pitt the Elder, later 1st Earl of Chatham, in 1761, and Thomas, Duke of Newcastle in 1762.

More so, as the war was still to be finished and the peace made. The dismissal of Pitt in particular helped greatly diminish George's public reputation as a 'Patriot King', but this verdict was unfair as the megalomaniacal Pitt, never willing to share collective responsibility, was an impossible figure as far as his colleagues were concerned. Yet politics, as George was to appreciate, is not about fairness, and he, not Pitt, was blamed, then and repeatedly later, for the ministry's failings.

George meanwhile devoted time to a key aspect of kingship: the maintenance of the dynasty. He had five siblings alive, three of them men, but all the men were unmarried (and, in the event, to die before George), as was George's sole paternal uncle, William, Duke of Cumberland; and bachelor monarchs were rarities. Like his father and grandfather, George sought a German Protestant princess, without the need his great-grandfather, George I, had had of the choice being fixed by the determination to consolidate the branches of the house of Brunswick-Lüneburg. A British choice, such as Lady Sarah Lennox, was not acceptable as George's wife would also be Electress of Hanover, and

German princely houses were highly concerned about issues of rank. The criteria George III employed centred on disposition and child-bearing ability; and factors for exclusion among those princesses initially considered included being too young, or having socially questionable marriages among ancestors, and being bad-tempered or inclined to secularism, or unlikely to have children. Charlotte of Mecklenburg-Strelitz (1744–1818) was eventually left alone in the field, and the difficulty of her being a Lutheran was ended when she expressed her readiness to conform to the Church of England. Allegedly a descendant of Alfonso III of Portugal and his African mistress, Charlotte has been called the first modern mixed-race royal, and comments on her 'mulatto' features have been made, but the basis for this thesis is problematic.

Mecklenburg, an area of Hanoverian concern and activity from the 1710s, did not offer a marriage at comparable rank, but of the other Electoral ruling houses, four (Bavaria, Bohemia, Palatinate and Saxony) were Catholic, and George broke with Prussia, the only other Protestant one, as an aspect of his change in policy when he negotiated peace at the close of the Seven Years War. Although the Peace of Paris did not come until 1763, George was critical of the deployment of British troops in Germany from 1758.

A Catholic bride from a royal house, the choice of Charles I and Charles II, was no longer politically possible in Britain. Instead, within this wider religious-political context, the criteria used were essentially those of compatibility. In terms of modern values, marriage to someone not previously met is scarcely the Western norm, but it was the custom of royalty then, and in modern cultures that follow the practice of arranged marriage there is often a search for what is assumed to lead to compatibility. They married on 8 September 1761, the day on which they met, and Philip, 4th Earl of Chesterfield commented four days later: 'The town of London and the city of Westminster are gone quite mad with the wedding and the approaching coronation.'[4] This, indeed, was a high point of popularity for the king.

With his irritable personality and emphasis on duty, George certainly could not have always been a relaxing spouse. Although they had similar views, there were to be some disagreements over the treatment of their daughters, and in later decades there were signs of tension; nevertheless, by the standards not only of the age but of any age, this was a successful marriage, certainly at least until the consequences of George's poor health hit hard after 1801. George and Charlotte had much in common: they enjoyed music-making and had a sexually active marriage, at least judged by the large number of children they produced, and there are plentiful signs of affection between them, as on George's return from Portsmouth in 1773:

> When he came to Kew he was so impatient to see the Queen that he opened the chaise himself and jumped out before any of his attendants could come to his assistance. He seized the Queen, whom he met at the door, round the waist, and carried her in his arms into the room.[5]

George did not go to Hanover and thus leave Charlotte, who was often pregnant, alone, and in later life they travelled together, including going on seaside breaks to Weymouth. They neither lived apart nor had affairs, as Charles II, James II, William III and George II all had done. Certainly until the 1800s, marriage gave George a stability and comfort he was not to find with all his children, and without the histrionics that later marked Victoria's response to Prince Albert.

With children born in 1762, 1763, 1765, 1766, 1767, 1768, 1770, 1771, 1773, 1774, 1776, 1777, 1779, 1780 and 1783, George was expanding his own immediate family. He spent a lot of time with Charlotte, and the Danish Secretary of Legation reported in 1771 that when they were in town, on days when the weather was fine and there were not court functions or council meetings, they went to Richmond and walked for a couple of hours in the garden.[6] Elizabeth, Duchess of Northumberland, one of Charlotte's ladies of the bedchamber, noted that the royal couple 'always dined Tete a Tete'.[7]

In contrast, the politics of the 1760s repeatedly proved dismal for the young king. Despite his great popularity on his accession and at his coronation as 'King of his united and unanimous people',[8] George soon became a figure of controversy because of his determination to reign without party and the implementation of this wish. As a result, the theme of the king as a dangerous political force exerting a malevolent role in British affairs, one long deployed by opponents of particular monarchs, was to be strongly revived in the 1760s and in a way that George had not anticipated.

In part, George's problems arose from inexperience, as he came to the throne young and had little earlier political grounding, but far more was involved: George, while being diligent, was not the brightest of monarchs in terms of the analysis of situations and possibilities. He was no pragmatist either, and was not willing to conform to the established nature of politics. Indeed, George had an agenda for Britain and, partly as a result, is politically the most interesting of the Hanoverians, for George I and George II had focused on foreign policy, often using Britain for Hanoverian ends. To many Whigs, accustomed under George I and George II to being the sole group in power, the novel practice of rejecting party government and seeking an inclusive political world, including Tory support for the ministry, was a revolutionary political step, almost an unconstitutional act on the part of the monarch. This response encouraged suspicions about George's intentions and, in the alarmist, frequently paranoid, political discussion of the period, offered an apparent echo of Stuart autocracy.

Throughout the reign, political opponents believed that George was out to increase royal power and that he acted in a manipulative way to do so, allegedly undermining politics by the use of secret advisers, or of ministers who were not committed to fair government. This group of supposed villains began with Bute, a key figure in George's contemporary and subsequent reputation, and came to include William, 1st Earl of Mansfield; Charles Jenkinson, later 1st Earl of Liverpool; William, 2nd Earl of Shelburne and later 1st Marquess of Lansdowne; Edward, Lord Thurlow; and William, Lord Auckland. This theme helped to inspire, and in turn drew heavily on, Edmund Burke's *Thoughts on the Cause of the Present Discontents* (1770), which became a key opposition text and would strongly influence nineteenth-century discussion of the reign.

What George did, or was reported to do, was perceived by many from this perspective. Thus in 1781 Christof Dreyer, the Danish envoy, noting George's determination to fight on after defeat by George Washington at the Battle of Yorktown, even at the risk of a fundamental political crisis, presented the government as manipulated by an 'interior Cabinet', many of them Scottish, that followed George's will; he repeated this analysis until the fall of the government the following spring.[9] The perception of secret influence accorded with a major theme, not only in the discussion of politics, in both the contemporary world and history, but also in fiction, and it was difficult to separate George from the apparent villainy of his advisers and their alleged intentions. Secret influence was closely aligned with conspiracy as a primary vehicle for explaining unforeseen events.

In practice, far from having unconstitutional tendencies, George saw himself as the constitution's defender; but his determination to deploy to the full powers that could be presented as his appeared to critics to be unconstitutional. Prone to see matters in black and white, he displayed a cool nerve in confrontations, total conviction of rectitude and a bloody-minded determination to have his way that flowed from the assumption that he alone was taking a principled stand. His tone of moral superiority and inflexibility often offended. Opponents of the king were enraged and spiteful and sought to constrain him by political pressure on his choice of ministers, conduct that matched that seen under previous monarchs. George, for his part, regarded this as unconstitutional.

Rather than acting in an unconstitutional fashion, George was a naïve idealist who, valuing integrity and fidelity, did not appreciate the nuances of politics and government. Equally, those nuances were defined and defended by self-serving politicians who were not easy to deal with, a description that (very differently) suited not only Pitt and Newcastle, but also George Grenville and Charles, 2nd Marquess of Rockingham. Patriotism as pursued by George, specifically the theme of a Patriot King able to unite all in the pursuit of national interests, proved, in fact, an aspiring ambience, rather than a practice of politics, and one that was ill suited to the British system, which, in this period, was – at once adversarial, institutional, populist and legalist – one that could flourish in the absence of a written constitution other than the ambiguous Bill of Rights. More than ministerial change was at issue, as George's policy reflected his support for the ideas and ideals of non-party government, not the Toryism alleged by his critics. Non-party government was quite a novelty in practice, one not really pursued since the time of Queen Anne. George also thought that much about the political system was corrupt and, in part, ascribed this to the size of the national debt; as a consequence, George's moral reformism, which drew on his strong personal piety, was specifically aimed against what he saw as faction and luxury. In the 1780s he was to support the Proclamation Society (which became the Society for the Suppression of Vice) and the various moral reform societies.

George's popularity rapidly diminished from late 1761 because of the break with Pitt over the minister's determination to dictate policy, George's reliance on Bute, dissatisfaction with the terms of the Peace of Paris of 1763 and hardship resulting from post-war fiscal policies, particularly the Cider Excise and the Stamp Act. The response to criticism also created issues, notably linked to the attacks in the press by the radical John Wilkes on George, Bute and the peace. Criticism brought not only the policies and attitudes of George into dispute, but also the power of the Crown, in the American colonies as well as Britain, leading the *salonnière* Elizabeth Montagu to pity George, 'who sees there is a determination in the great factions to make him their slave'.[10]

At the same time, alongside the pronounced partisan froth and readily apparent ministerial instability of the decade, George was gaining in experience. As leading figures from the previous reign died – Granville in 1763, both Philip, 1st Earl of Hardwicke and William, 1st Earl of Bath in 1764, Cumberland in 1765 and Newcastle in 1768 – he felt less hedged in. Although George found it difficult, the collapse of Bute's influence from 1763, both politically and over him, was also important to the king's recovery in popularity, while he was more adroit than he had been in the early 1760s. It is inaccurate, as well as too easy, to draw a direct line from the disorder in British politics in the 1760s to the chaos of the years of the War of American Independence.

George certainly lessened tension by being far less focused than his two predecessors on the Electorate of Hanover. As prince, George had criticized this partiality and the related

continental interventionism in British foreign policy, both
the commitment to Hanover and alliance with Prussia;
instead, colonial, commercial and maritime issues came to
the fore in foreign policy during his reign. The break with
his grandfather's ministers was intertwined with the break
with the policies of the 1750s: it was not only that the alliance with Prussia was abandoned in 1762 as a prelude to
the end of the war, but also that, despite negotiations, the
gap was not filled by an alliance with another major continental power. The motives for such an alliance – royal
anxiety about Hanover, ministerial concern about this
anxiety, and the sense that defensive arrangements for
Hanover could, and should, serve as the basis for a British
alliance system – had been largely lost. So also, in the turn
towards a more prudent understanding of British interests
and commitments, had the interventionist habit of mind and
the concomitant diplomatic assumptions. In 1761, Baron
Haslang, the experienced Wittelsbach envoy, noted that
there would be no return of British conquests from France
in order to make gains for Hanover.[11] Nevertheless, George
abandoned the idea, considered by his predecessors, of
separating Hanover from Britain. His testament of 1765
established the succession of George, his firstborn, the
future George IV, as heir to both.

By the late 1760s, George no longer had illusions about
promoting a new political culture in Britain, focusing more
narrowly on the still-ambitious task of charting a path
between ministerial factions to create a ministry with
which he could be comfortable. In the absence of parties
with clear leadership on the modern pattern, let alone with

a nationwide organization, it should have been possible for George to create a ministry around the politician most acceptable to him who might be able to manage Parliament and, conversely, to keep at a distance those whom he disliked. Even if George had to accept ministers who were not his first choice (as in 1763, 1765, 1782, 1783, 1804 and 1806), it was possible for him to try to use a ministry that could manage Parliament in order to win support for royal interests.

George found this difficult, both because there was no longer the binding of Whig ministers to the monarch that stemmed from a fear of Jacobitism as from 1714 to the late 1740s, but also as his accession was followed by a more troubling agenda in domestic and imperial politics. George was associated with domestic issues that were contentious in their own right, and in which the role of the monarch was particularly sensitive, or appeared so: in the 1760s, this was true of his choice of ministers and, from 1765, of policy on the North American colonies. The king therefore took a close interest in politics.

He found it challenging to establish and sustain a stable ministry. When in office, as First Lord of the Treasury in 1762–3, Bute proved a broken reed, better with abstract ideas than with the realities of political management, and the unpopularity of the minister cast a shadow over the public reputation of the monarch. In turn, George Grenville, who was First Lord of the Treasury in 1763–5, had poor relations with the king, whom he was prone to hector. Neither man managed the clash in their natures well. However disagreeable personally, the ministry was pursuing policies dear to George, especially peace and fiscal stability, and Grenville was a competent minister and administrator.

Order and decorum were also conspicuously at stake for George when he fully supported the ministry in its clash with John Wilkes. In governmental eyes, this dispute was an attempt to enforce constitutional propriety and royal and ministerial dignity. Wilkes, a libertine MP and an entrepreneur of faction, fell foul of his antithesis, George, as a result of bitter attacks on the government in his newspaper the *North Briton*, which sought to exploit dissatisfaction in the capital. George, who viewed Wilkes (like so much else) through a moral as well as a political lens, hated him because of his veiled reference to Augusta and Bute as lovers, while his denunciation of the Peace of Paris in number 45, issued on 23 April 1763, with its implication that George had lied in his speech from the throne, led to a charge of seditious libel.

The government in turn faced a crisis stemming from colonial taxation. The Stamp Act of 1765, which was pressed by George, who played a significant role in supporting the policy of taxing the colonies to support the troops there,[12] was opposed by the colonists. George was not prepared to force his will, in the shape of his opposition to concession, on his new ministry, that of Charles, 2nd Marquess of Rockingham, First Lord of the Treasury in 1765–6, a protégé of Newcastle. Indeed, the ministry was able to use George's influence to secure the agreement of the House of Lords to the repeal of the Stamp Act. However, George was unhappy about being head of a government which would not follow views he thought acceptable and necessary; and this feeling contributed to an impression of distance that was seen clearly when he complained about his ministers, both during the Rockingham ministry and on other occasions. Indeed, George was apt to be aggrieved if his opinions and goodwill were not reciprocated; and reciprocation, in his eyes, tended to entail agreement, which was a matter of his personality and his interpretation of the relationship between Patriot kingship and politicians. In 1766, George failed to sustain Rockingham when the ministry faced division over the position of Catholics in the new conquest of Québec. Instead he turned to Pitt, but doing so did not bring him the popular support he had forfeited when Pitt had resigned in 1761. Moreover, amid the complexities of peacetime politics, the sense of national unity that Pitt had been able to benefit from and to foster during the Seven Years War, and that George had sought to redefine and redirect, was absent.

Created Earl of Chatham in July 1766, Pitt neither took the task of leading the Commons nor accepted one of the major offices of business. Repeating George's mistaken expectation that good men would come together on a non-party basis to further national interests, and facing stress and depression, Chatham became an invalid, and George turned in 1768 to Chatham's ally Augustus, 3rd Duke of Grafton, who had become First Lord of the Treasury in 1766.

George continued to take an active role in the details of politics, notably being fired up with anger by Wilkes, who was elected for Middlesex in the general election of 1768. George successfully pressed the Cabinet to have Wilkes expelled from the Commons, a step that was to expose the government to considerable embarrassment, although given Wilkes's irreligion the Commons would probably have rejected him without royal pressure. Three times re-elected in 1769, Wilkes was rejected by the Commons each time. Wilkes was also the focus of more widespread popular opposition to the government and of a measure of radicalism that led, in 1768, to a series of riots in London, which included criticism of George for failing to respond to the Wilkesite petitions. Relations between George and the City of London became particularly poor, and his dismissive responses to City remonstrances were criticized.

Despite their different religious sympathies (Grafton was more liberal), George liked him, but the duke, who faced both political criticism and the problems of his divorce, was not really up to the job, either as a minister or as a politician. In January 1770, he resigned when Chatham went into opposition and the opposition groups joined forces. At the start of the new decade, ministerial stability appeared as elusive as ever.

3
An Interlude of Peace

The King is exceeding delighted with his reception at Portsmouth. He said to a person about that he was convinced he was not so unpopular as the newspapers would represent him to be. The acclamations of the people were indeed prodigious. On his return all the country assembled in the towns where he changed horses. At Godalming every man had a branch of a tree in his hand and every woman a nosegay which they presented to the King (the horses moving as slow as possible) till he was up to the knees in flowers, and they all singing in a tumultuous manner, God Save the King. The King was so affected that he could not refrain shedding abundance of tears, and even joined in the chorus.[1]

Joshua Reynolds's comments on George's return from the review of the fleet in 1773 were complemented by that of the MP Hans Stanley, who did not see the awkward shyness presented in modern caricatures:

I knew him sufficiently before, to be persuaded that he did not want either politeness, or a certain degree of play and imagination in conversation, but as he has lived so much in retirement, I thought he would have been embarrassed and reserved in so large a company . . . but Charles II could not have been more affable, more easy, or more engaging at his table, and would not have had so much discretion and propriety; I did not attend him in his survey of the docks . . . but I am told his questions were all manly, sensible, and pertinent, and that he made every note and observation, from whence this expedition might be a real instruction to him, and not a mere amusement.[2]

Portsmouth was a special case, with huge numbers of its inhabitants directly dependent on the Crown, while any royal association with the navy was popular, and this was to be shown anew when George visited the base again in 1778. However, the account of the response on the journey back is instructive, and suggests that the usual chronology for shifts in George's popularity – a decline following Pitt's resignation in 1761 and a revival from 1784 – requires revision. In London there were still certainly signs of unpopularity: George was hissed when he drove to Parliament in 1771, and an apple was thrown at his carriage, but the extent of his unpopularity outside London needs to be qualified. Indeed, in October 1778, by when Britain was at war with France, George noted his 'thorough satisfaction at the manner in which I have been received by all ranks of people on my late tour'.[3]

The political situation had stabilized when George replaced the unenthusiastic Grafton with a ministry under Frederick, Lord North on 28 January 1770. At last, he had found a first minister able to lead the Commons, manage business and maintain a more united government. There was a personal link as North's father, one of Frederick, Prince of Wales's lords of the bedchamber, had been Prince George's first governor, being replaced only when Frederick died. An MP from 1754, North was six years older than George, a talented Treasury minister and, to the king, a sound man whom he could trust, although he was later to complain that he found him indecisive.

North was helped by a natural rallying of support to the Crown, the focus of most politicians' loyalty, that took place in response both to the extremism of some of the opposition and to a more general concern about the preservation of order. Furthermore, the reintegration of the Tories into the political mainstream in the late 1750s and the 1760s, however much a cause of criticism of George, helped heal a long-standing divide dating from the mid seventeenth century that had posed a challenge to political stability. North himself was an experienced and astute politician and capable Chancellor of the Exchequer, and a good-tempered and courteous individual with whom George felt relaxed, not least as the two men shared a devout Anglicanism and a commitment to family. George bestowed the Order of the Garter on North in 1772 and paid his debts in 1777, which the king regretted when they later fell out over 1780 election expenses.[4]

North proved an active minister, at least until 1778–9, but George continued to keep a close eye on politics, and his correspondence is a testimony to his engagement. Parliament was a particular focus of attention and co-operation: North wrote regular parliamentary reports for George and was pressed by the king, who took a detailed interest in division figures, to win over or inspire particular parliamentarians. Signs of a more widespread popularity for the government were certainly seen in the satisfactory results in the general elections of 1774 and 1780.

George regarded royal office as a welcome duty that provided him with an opportunity to exercise his responsibilities, and duty, diligence and precision had ensured that he had acquired considerable knowledge of politics and of much else. Indeed, knowing that he had done his duty was important to George, particularly in crises, an approach that reflected his personal piety and was the product of a sense of Christian kingship that drew both on British examples and German pietism. Agostino Carlini captured this resolution in his 1773 marble bust of the king, while duty also stands out from George's copious correspondence. Yet, although a prig, George was tolerant in religious terms, for example visiting the Catholic chapel of Thomas Weld of Lulworth Castle while his guest in Dorset in 1789 and 1791. In 1778 he had stayed at Thorndon Hall, the seat of Robert, Lord Petre, a prominent Catholic peer.

Conscientiousness guided George in his attitude to others, not least his conviction that personal merit was crucial to appointment, promotion and conduct in both Church and state. George took his responsibilities in appointments seriously, and was opposed to 'personal jobs' and 'favour' and to promising what was not yet vacant; although he was put under a lot of pressure by his ministers over state appointments. His reluctance to award unmerited patronage extended even to his family. Increasingly, George had more knowledge and experience than some of his ministers.

In 1771 he told Sir Stanier Porten, an under-secretary, of his conviction that government offices must ensure 'regularity and secrecy . . . clearness essentially necessary. System and secrecy the fundamentals of offices. Disliked circulation, believed few read papers themselves, at least few could enter into discourse with him on any matter.' Having had a ninety-minute audience on his return in 1787 from northern Europe, Sir John Sinclair 'was astonished with the extent of information which the King displayed upon a variety of subjects'.[5] In 1793, reading 'with great attention' a draft declaration to the French nation by William, Lord Grenville, the Foreign Secretary, George corrected both the copyist and the original.[6]

Conscientiousness and the sense of responsibility that the king strove to inculcate in his children can be related not only to his piety and sense of morality, but also to his mental health. In the mid twentieth century, at a time when personality traits were linked to psychiatric conditions, not least repressed sexuality, there was a widespread failure to consider the relationship between mental illness and physical causes. One American psychiatrist discerned 'manic-depressive insanity' arising from an inability to tolerate his own timorous uncertainty.[7] Subsequently, there was a shift in psychiatry towards looking more closely at the relationship between mental disorder and physical health, and a focus on the effects on George of the disease porphyria. That shift also went too far, and there was insufficient attention to his mental state during the bulk of his reign, when he was not ill. Noting four bouts of mania, it is possible that George suffered from manic depression,[8] which would account for his compulsive characteristics, although much should also be attributed to his hard-working interpretation of the *métier* of kingship.

No simple explanation is satisfactory: George's desire for order may have owed something to his personality, or even to his concern about his own irritable anxiety when faced with disorder, but his beliefs about his role are also pertinent. An emphasis on order certainly affected George's relations with his family, not least with his three brothers, who were very different from George in personality and behaviour, notably Henry, Duke of Cumberland (1745–90); this underlines the need not to place too great an emphasis on clashes between the generations. In 1770, George had to lend Cumberland the money he owed as a result of an affair with Harriet, Lady Grosvenor, and in 1771 the duke had a clandestine marriage with a commoner. The furious George, who failed to get Cumberland to disavow the marriage, barred him from his presence, and actively sponsored the Royal Marriages Act of 1772, which gave the king a position of legal authority over his family's marriages. The minority of peers who opposed the legislation presented it as an infringement of constitutional values.

Under the act, descendants of George II, with the exception of the descendants of princesses who married abroad, could only marry before the age of twenty-five with royal permission. Thereafter, they had to give a year's notice to the Privy Council, and Parliament had not expressly to disapprove of the marriage. George, Prince of Wales's secret marriage of 1785 to Maria Fitzherbert was in defiance of this act, as well as of the 1701 Act of Settlement because she was a Catholic. When he was informed that a favourite son, Augustus, had married the pregnant Lady Augusta Murray in 1793, George ordered the government to proceed in accordance with the Royal Marriages Act, and the marriage was declared void the following year. Meanwhile, Cumberland and William, Duke of Gloucester, who had also married secretly, had not been received at court until 1780 when the offer of help in the Gordon Riots changed the king's attitude; even thereafter, their wives were never received.

Meanwhile, in his artistic patronage George had moved from his earlier focus on Italianate work, on the purchase of which he had spent heavily in 1762–3, to add more classical and national themes. His admiration for Poussin and the classical inheritance led him to commission 'history works', moral accounts of classical episodes, including *Timon of Athens* from Nathaniel Dance in 1765 and *The Departure of Regulus* from Benjamin West in 1768, which was a widespread artistic preference of the period, reflecting the notion that culture should be exemplary: Timon rejected luxury and Regulus was a self-sacrificing hero of Republican Rome. He appointed Benjamin West Historical Painter to the King in 1772 and gave him much patronage. Culture was linked to patriotism in the foundation of the Royal Academy in 1768, which George helped finance and which he honoured by knighting its president, Joshua Reynolds, in 1769. George was also a key patron of Thomas Gainsborough, from whom he commissioned a series of portraits of the royal family which were artistically bold, as Gainsborough's sparing use of paint was less fashionable than Reynolds's habit of slapping it on. George, who was called 'a good connoisseur' by Gainsborough,[9] also favoured Paul Sandby, a master of the watercolour.

George took a keen interest in the theatre, both in London and on his tours, and was fond of music. He played the flute, harpsichord (frequently) and pianoforte, and collected music, including works by Lully, Palestrina and Scarlatti. He also actively amassed copies and arrangements of Handel's oratorios in the 1760s, and in the early 1770s was presented by Handel's amanuensis, John Smith, with the composer's manuscript scores and harpsichord. In the 1780s he patronized the revival of Handel's oratorios – with their religious themes – but not the operas.

Spending a lot of money on his library, George was particularly interested in books on theology, history, jurisprudence, science, the arts and the classical inheritance; less so in fiction. Meeting Samuel Johnson in 1767, the king was able to discuss books of sermons with him, George praising seventeenth-century writers such as Robert Sanderson, a chaplain to and a favourite preacher of Charles I, who lost his living and the divinity chair at Oxford because he refused to subscribe to the Parliamentarians' Solemn League and Covenant. Johnson both advised on the purchase of books for the royal family and was a beneficiary of the largesse of the king, who also appointed the prominent historian William Robertson Historiographer Royal in Scotland.

George was deeply interested in the past, and, to a degree, reverential of it, while he was reflective when he visited the

tomb of the overthrown and murdered Edward II in Gloucester Cathedral in 1788. When his brother Henry married a
commoner in 1771, the outraged and overwrought George
informed another brother, William, that such a step might
threaten civil war, as he claimed that the fifteenth-century
Wars of the Roses owed much to the intermarriage of
Crown and nobility.[10] George also took a clear view on
legitimacy that made allowance for the cause of the Stuarts, an allowance that extended from 1799 to providing
financial support for 'Henry IX', the younger son of 'James
III', who succeeded to the Jacobite claim in 1788 and was
a cardinal and therefore not in a position to continue the
claim. George had no time for the false report that 'James
III', the 'warming-pan baby' of 1688, was a changeling.

George saw his position and that of future British monarchs as resting not solely on dynastic right, but on duty.
Mindful of what the Glorious Revolution of 1688 meant in
terms of the rejection of unacceptable monarchy, George
argued that it had rescued Britain 'from the iron rod of
arbitrary power', while, separately, distinguishing those in
opposition to Charles I 'who, not content with removing
abuses, were for removing foundations'.[11] In 1799, an over-
ture on behalf of 'Henry IX', whose property had been
seized by the French, led George to reflect that he had 'ever
thought that the true solid basis' of Hanoverian rule was
that 'it came to preserve the free constitution of this empire,
both in church and state, which compact I trust none of my
successors will ever dare to depart from.'[12] George's linkage
of Church and state chimed strongly with such contemporaries as Johnson and Edmund Burke. In contrast, for the

Whigs, both then and later, it was possible to locate George III and George IV as opponents of reform, villains who were later versions of the dastardly Stuarts.

Like his father, George, who had been taught physics and chemistry as a boy, was interested in science. Naturally inquisitive, and displaying an eclectic intelligence which had the insight to appreciate the ideas of those he recognized as more learned than himself, George revived royal links with the Royal Society and collected scientific instruments. Princess Augusta showed how well she knew her son when she had Chambers design the King's Observatory as a gift to enable him to watch the transit of Venus in 1769. When he visited Oxford in 1785, George went to the observatory there. Always interested in how things were made, and in making them himself, George, after touring Portsmouth in 1773, pressed for details on how ropes were made for the navy.[13]

George's engagement with watches, clocks, astronomy, botany and the music of Handel has been attributed to a striving to take refuge from the pressures of his personality in obsessive intellectual activities centring on the clear demonstration of order and regularity.[14] This is argument by assertion, and reductive, ignoring in particular the role of individual interest and general fashion. Astronomy, botany and the accurate measurement of time and longitude were all beneficiaries of the latter, and many who shared in this interest presumably did not have George's psychological profile. Was George's zest for hunting a desire to escape the travails of his life, a preference for open-air pursuits, the product of a frustrated desire to command, a substitute for military activity, or something else? Louis XVI matched George's interest in hunting, botany, watches and clocks, but had a very different personality.

As far as the arts and sciences are concerned, it is best to note George's role not as a spectator but as an informed and committed patron, with wide-ranging cultural and intellectual interests and a desire to become engaged, as he showed in his performance of music. He made available the royal apartments in Somerset House for the Royal Academy from 1771, and although, like most monarchs, he is not usually regarded as an intellectual, George was interested in the arts and sciences in a way that his two predecessors were not.

Fundamental to his perception of kingship, George was an active supporter of the Church of England, with a strong faith, unlike his father, grandfather and great-grandfather. The promise of 'endless bliss' after death was real to the king, as was gratitude to the 'Great Preserver', ever present and watchful. George's dependence for salvation on divine mercy, not on human merit, was accompanied by a belief in the need to show thanks for the divine gift of life by means of appropriate conduct. These beliefs guided George's own conduct and helped structure his time. Sundays were special to him and he tried not to handle government business, while court life deferred to religious duty, and no levees, drawing rooms or card-playing were held during Passion or Whit weeks. George repeatedly saw divine intervention at work in the affairs of man, and awareness of God and divine injunctions as being a particular guide to monarchs and, linked to that, a duty and a responsibility.

George made religious issues even more central in politics than they might otherwise have been, and helped ensure that those of the Anglican devout who had been uneasy about the Glorious Revolution and the Hanoverian succession rallied to the Crown, strengthening the identity both of the Church of England and of the nation, which matched (and was linked to) the political reconciliation with the Tories. In turn, a Dissenter challenge to the new order developed, one that George resisted, as in 1772 when he opposed the Feathers Tavern petition, an unsuccessful attempt to end Anglican clerical subscription to the Thirty-Nine Articles as a necessary precondition for becoming graduates or clerics. The American War of Independence would only strengthen his concerns about heterodoxy.

4
American Debacle

One of George's strengths was that he instinctually knew what his duty was, but a major weakness was that this conviction was not always illuminated by careful reflection, and could therefore seem both obtuse and stubborn. In practice, he was critical of those who tried to temper what he thought appropriate, and the attitudes that established his response to the American Patriots were already set before the outbreak of the war there. The American War of Independence (1775–83) tends to assume a disproportionate role in his reputation, and the multitude of charges thrown incontinently at George by Thomas Jefferson in the Declaration of Independence of 1776 focused not on the British monarchy but on George himself, the charge-sheet beginning:

> The history of the present King of Great Britain is a history
> of unremitting injuries and usurpations, all having in direct
> object the establishment of an absolute tyranny over these
> States . . . He has refused his assent to laws the most whole-
> some and necessary for the public good.

George's determination to maintain royal authority certainly played a major role in the breakdown in relations

with the American colonies. Already, in the Stamp Act crisis of 1765–6, George had been

> more and more grieved at the accounts from America.
> Where this spirit will end is not to be said; it is undoubtedly
> the most serious matter that ever came before Parliament. It
> requires more deliberation, candour and temper than I fear
> it will meet with.[1]

George's political moves within Britain had already helped
to spawn a critical political literature that in part influenced the American response to successive ministerial plans
to increase American revenues, or to maintain control in the
colonies. There was widespread colonial concern about the
ministerial view, supported by George, that the colonists
should pay for their security; but initially the blame focused
on the ministers, and George for long retained much of his
popularity in America.

By 1774, however, George's reputation among Anglo-
Americans in North America was under great pressure,
which was a result not so much of the impact there of the
domestic British critique of his supposed autocratic policies, but of the actual measures being followed in America
in order to sustain the furthering of the integrated imperial
policy. Indeed, the revolution occurred not because of a
general desire to fight for liberty, but rather as a hesitant,
if not unwilling, response on the part of many to the con-
fused tergiversations of British policy, policy changes that
apparently pointed the way to new forms of imperial governance. This concern led in the colonies to a depth of

alienation that was underrated in Britain, at least by the government, or that was misleadingly seen as restricted to a few troublemakers. Separation was a last resort for most of the colonists.

A lack of understanding of American colonial society and aspirations on the part of the imperial government, not least George and North, played a major role in the developing crisis. George might have had 'so perfect a knowledge of the state of his dominions',[2] but he did not grasp the degree to which the individual colonies were joining together in response to successive crises, making joint action on the part of the colonies increasingly an option. This failure of appreciation was exacerbated in 1774 by the view that concessions would be seen as weakness and lead only to fresh demands. Shocked by the Boston Tea Party on 16 December 1773, George supported a firm line, as he saw the status quo as no longer an option, matters as beyond compromise, and leniency as destructive of order and good government. The legislation of early 1774, the Coercive (or Intolerable) Acts, designed to punish Massachusetts, struck colonists as an infringement of their charter rights; but the general election in Britain, held from 5 October to 10 November, sustained the position of the North ministry. George opposed any suspension of the Coercive Acts, a very widely shared conviction strengthened by his belief that the repeal in 1766 of the Stamp Act of 1765 had caused many of the problems in North America. Moreover, committed to the constitution and to a view of the necessary political, economic and ideological interdependence of the empire, George was not going to veto parliamentary legislation that affected American rights and interests, the course urged by Jefferson. The king wrote to North, 'the die is now cast, the colonies must either submit or triumph,' later adding, 'The New England governments are in a state of rebellion ... blows must decide whether they are to be subject to this country or independent.'[3] The collapse of authority appeared to menace Britain's position as a great power and to threaten internal dissidence.

As we have seen, duty, legality and order were crucial to George's politico-moral assumptions, and he referred to the American Patriots in 1775 as 'rebellious children', which was the standard response to disaffection in monarchies in which the personal role of the ruler remained central, and a total contrast to Tom Paine's view of him in *Common Sense* (1776) as a bad parent. On 26 October 1775, opening a new parliamentary session, George undermined American moderates by rejecting conciliation, a measure advocated by a large section of British opinion. Instead, coercion was to come first, George declaring that it was necessary 'to put a speedy end to these disorders by the most decisive exertions'. In judging George's views, it helps to avoid the traps of hindsight and the prejudices of the Whigs.

A very different view to that of the Whigs was offered by John Wesley's far from short but commercially very successful *Concise History of England*, also published in 1776, which adopted the view of monarchy as an ideal form that was opposed by the follies of party government. James I was criticized by Wesley for not acting 'as a plain, country gentleman would have acted towards his tenants upon his private estate',[4] an idealization of a monarch serving in a paternalist

and patriotic fashion that captured the theme of both
Bolingbroke's *The Idea of a Patriot King* (1740) and George,
and also, unintentionally, the degree of unreality bound
up in it. George was able to present the role, but, to an
extent, it shaded into a Tory rejection of the modern world as
almost inherently corrupt and a call, in contrast, for a return
to a simpler society. However benign, the attitude did not
generate policies adequate to cope with the crisis in North
America. Indeed, the fiscal policies of George and his
ministers rested on a failure to understand American circumstances, and also challenged political assumptions
about the need for consent from colonies dominated by
British settlers.

In the time George II spent in Hanover in 1736, George
III could have easily got to Boston, New York or Philadelphia and back. That was not a prospect, but it is unclear
how far George's views would have changed had he seen
more of the empire, for, in April 1775, George was unwilling
to hear a pro-American petition from the livery of London
while sitting on the throne; while, in response to the Olive
Branch Petition, in which Congress declared a wish to
remain in the empire, but also underlined their conviction
of the justness of their cause in protection of their constitutional liberties, George adopted the legalistic position of
rejecting it because Congress had no legal status and
indeed was composed of rebels. This stance greatly helped
undermine moderate American Patriots, who did not wish
to move from resistance to independence, leaving them no
alternative but war. That George's assumptions were in
line with contemporary Spanish, Portuguese and French

policies indicates that the king was not exceptionally foolish or wicked, but in retrospect it was a serious mistake.

To the colonists there was, in the government's attitude, a
dangerous departure from earlier patterns. The British Parliament was working out a theory and practice of the unified
sovereignty over the empire of the king-in-Parliament; the
Americans, in contrast, had no initial problem with royal
sovereignty, but were clear that the king should tax them
through their own assemblies, rather than through the
Westminster Parliament. It is insufficiently appreciated that
it was the latter that had everything to lose from this American formulation, and not George. Indeed, rebutting Charles
James Fox's claim that the ministry was Tory, North declared
in the Commons on 26 October 1775 that the 'aim of Toryism was to increase the prerogative. That in the present case,
the administration contended for the right of Parliament,
while the Americans talked of belonging to the Crown.'[5]
Despite charges that his intentions were despotic, George
was not interested in the radical option of rejecting the
pretensions of the Westminster Parliament and negotiat-
ing directly with the colonial legislatures. Indeed, it was
the Americans who wanted George to act unconstitution-
ally in order to protect their rights.[6]

The outbreak of fighting on 19 April 1775, at Concord
and Lexington, meant that George could be seen as using
British forces to kill subjects, in short as a monarch of evil
intent and action, and the listing in the Declaration of
Independence of what Samuel Adams termed George's 'catalogue of crimes' was the indictment of a monarch who had
misused his executive powers as well as combining with

Parliament to attack American liberties. By appearing to be reasonable revolutionaries and portraying George as a tyrant, the Patriots both justified their actions and sought to appeal to the support of France and Spain, which were monarchies. The list also accused him of waging war in a cruel fashion, and some of the language was even biblical, likening George to an Old Testament plague.

In response to British actions, there was a powerful symbolic break that focused on George and had a lasting impact on his reputation. On 9 July 1776, the inhabitants of New York City pulled down a gilded equestrian statue of the king erected on Bowling Green in 1770 (its metal was to be used for musket cartridges), while, more generally, the royal arms were taken down and usually treated with contempt. The king's name was removed from governmental and legal documents, royal portraits were reversed or destroyed, and he was subjected to mock trials, executions and funerals, each a potent rejection of his authority. Streets and buildings were renamed, King's College in New York becoming Columbia, although King's Chapel survived in Boston.

Once fighting broke out, George kept a close eye on details of activities linked to the war, as was clearly shown in his correspondence with John Robinson, the secretary to the Treasury, and gave his advice on military planning. Domestic criticism of the war did not encourage George to desist, and he instead linked the maintenance of authority in America to that in Britain. North's attempts to strengthen the ministry by bringing in opposition leaders met with George's determination to thwart negotiations unless the leaders agreed to strive to keep the empire complete. In 1778, the war broadened when France came in on the side of the Americans, Spain following in 1779. George associated himself with the war effort by visiting the naval dockyards at Chatham and a crowded Portsmouth, where the fleet was fitting out, as well as military encampments. As a result, he was seen by a large number of his subjects. In 1780, the exhibition of the Royal Academy displayed Benjamin West's resolute *Portrait of His Majesty* (1779), showing George in military uniform and holding a document. In 1779, a sense of national emergency led George to consider the distribution of pikes in the face of threatened invasion.

Ministers were individually responsible to George and to Parliament, ensuring that he was effectively head of the Cabinet when occasion demanded it; but he did not habitually preside at Cabinet and left the business of government to ministers. George lobbied his ministers to remain loyal, but, faced with the consequences of the fundamental lack of Cabinet cohesion, and finding it hard to manage the situation, North repeatedly asked to retire, only to meet with refusal from the king, who did not want a change in personnel or measures, despite being irritated by North. Instead, George emphasized willpower and fortitude, seeing the latter as a religious quality and duty. His attitude might seem an impressive display of tenacity and resolve were it not based on a flawed assessment of the military and political situation in America. George understood the distinction between battle and war, and appreciated that victory in the former would not necessarily guarantee success in the latter, but he underestimated the difficulty of getting the Americans to accept that they might have lost sufficiently to ensure negotiations, and also failed to grasp the depths of the strategic dilemma posed by Bourbon entry into the war. His politics ensured that the war could not be reconceptualized as a struggle with the Bourbons, the course urged by the opposition, and one that would have freed the British from the strategic incubus of conflict in America, for George was still determined to defeat the Americans.

Like so many of his contemporaries, George trusted in Divine Providence, notably in 1779 when Britain was facing the prospect of Bourbon invasion. George's emphasis on the desirability of moral behaviour was not the imposition of piety on an amoral, secular culture, but the bringing together of two powerful currents: the ideal of a Christian people led by a Christian king, and the need to ensure that society and the common good were preserved from the inroads of corruption. It was also possibly a response to the growing millenarianism which suggested that the end of the world was approaching, a view very much held by Richard Hurd, Bishop of Lichfield, whom George admired. The ability to heed the call of duty was necessary not only for the king but also for his subjects if they were to avoid a fall into savagery, a view that brought together Christian notions of sinfulness, Patriot anxieties about corruptibility, and anthropological assessments of a hierarchical differentiation of peoples. Indeed, in 1780 George referred to 'the strange, wild and wicked conduct of Opposition'.[7]

It is tempting to press on with the narrative of the war, but to do so ignores the extent to which any biography necessarily involves a simultaneity of goals and experiences, and separating these out into distinct strands is seriously misleading. During the war, which happened in an environment made more distant by the time taken for dispatches to cross the Atlantic, George was of course involved in much else. Although not a builder on the scale of his son George IV, or of such contemporaries as Catherine the Great of Russia, in large part because he believed in restraining expenditure, George was interested in architecture and a leading patron.[8] He neglected some of the existing palaces, notably Hampton Court and Kensington Palace, both of which were allocated to others, and St James's Palace, which was now largely the setting for royal ceremonial, notably drawing rooms and levees. Instead, when in London, George focused on the Queen's House, which he had purchased in 1762 and which he had considerably altered by Chambers. By 1774, £73,000 had been spent on building and redecoration there. Built in 1702–5 for John, 1st Duke of Buckingham, and the core of what is now Buckingham Palace, the Queen's House included many baroque features that George found unwelcome, such as a row of statues on the skyline and angle pilasters. These were removed, and the neo-classical style was accentuated, with a pediment over the front door, while other additions included four library rooms and the riding house. From the king's bedroom, a door led directly into the great library. Function was not incompatible with grandeur, as the entrance hall and saloon at the Queen's House demonstrated, but George's apartments were relatively plain, and certainly not lavish.

George's first country residence, Richmond Lodge, was

to be demolished, having been judged too small for his rapidly growing family. He turned to the White House in Kew,
the country home of his parents, but wanted a new palace
in the area; initially at Richmond, for which, in 1765,
Chambers produced a design for a major neo-classical work
in accordance with the traditions of country-house (i.e.
rural-palace) building associated with Colen Campbell
and William Kent. The main façade was to be 328 feet long,
but this was never built because, in contradiction to the
Declaration of Independence, George was no tyrant: the
cost was too great for the modest royal finances. Also,
he was unable to purchase some land adjacent to his property which he saw as necessary for the palace, and certainly
could not expropriate it as he very much regarded himself
as under the law. In 1770 construction started on a more
modest palace, but it was abandoned in 1775, and in 1776
George decided to use Queen's Lodge at Windsor as a personal residence, which would be enlarged and upgraded to
fit the entire royal family.

Meanwhile, George faced growing pressure for political
reform in Britain. The nature of elections was an issue, as
was expenditure on the Crown, and opposition politicians
attacked as corrupt the Civil List, which funded government pensions (annual payments) as well as some royal
expenditure. On 6 April 1780, against ministerial wishes,
the House of Commons passed a resolution proposed by
John Dunning, MP for Calne: 'The influence of the Crown
has increased, is increasing, and ought to be diminished.'
This was followed by a successful motion to investigate
Civil List expenditure. The attack on the royal position

was a response to George's role in keeping the ministry behind the American war, but ensured that the king was even more resolved to question the opposition's motives and to block them from office.

In June 1780, George faced a very different challenge in the shape of the Gordon Riots in London, which arose because of anger about measures to ease the legal position for Catholics. In the ensuing violence George pressed for resolution, and, whereas the magistrates panicked and refused to act, the unflustered king remained firm. 'Convinced till the magistrates have ordered some military execution on the rioters this town will not be restored to order,'[9] George summoned the Privy Council, which empowered the army to employ force without the prior permission of a magistrate. George was then instrumental in the deployment and use of the troops that ended the crisis.

After that, George was unwilling to pander to the strength of popular anti-Catholicism by making concessions. His attitudes and policies did not clash with his subsequent opposition to Catholic Emancipation because, to him, an emphasis on amelioration did not compromise his responsibilities as head of the established Church. Furthermore, with his sense of duty, George did not see himself as a populist: he was ready both to oppose bigotry in 1780 and to sustain discrimination in the 1790s and 1800s, and did not regard these as contradictory.

The reaction against the Gordon Riots helped the government temporarily to recover the initiative against popular politics, which were now associated with disorder. In turn, domestic political difficulties in Britain were kept at bay as a result of success in the 1780 general election, which was held from 6 September to 18 October. However, military failure in America was to plunge the political system into crisis. Surrender of an army under Charles, 2nd Earl Cornwallis at Yorktown on 19 October 1781 led to a crisis of confidence in Parliament that brought down the North ministry in March 1782, beginning a period of serious instability that lasted until 1784. George's reluctance to negotiate peace undermined the chance of keeping a reconstituted North ministry in power. Instead, with North insisting on resigning, George was forced to turn to the Rockinghamites and to accept that peace would entail the abandonment of the colonies. Faced by the collapse of his expectations and hopes, the king even drafted an abdication speech in which he announced he would move to Hanover, but it was never delivered.

Nor did he ever go to Hanover. Alongside his Englishness, he was Elector of Hanover, with German parents and a German wife, and he continued to play a part in German politics, as well as sending six of his sons to be educated there. The German connection even gave him an extra dimension in English politics, using Germans as a secret means of communicating with English politicians against a hostile government in 1783, and Hanoverian diplomatic information as an extra weapon in debates with his ministers on foreign policy. In 1786, George told the visiting novelist Sophie von La Roche: 'my heart will never forget that it pulses with German blood.'[10] He spoke German with envoys who knew the language and continued his predecessor's close links with the Hanoverian Chancery in London, in effect the governmental office there for Hanover. Indeed, George showed stronger interest in Hanover in the 1780s than previously, in part due to concern about the pretensions and aggressiveness of Emperor Joseph II, which threatened his opposition to change in the Empire; but also due to his frustration with the political situation in Britain.

Succeeding North in 1782, Rockingham obliged George to agree to unwelcome terms, including acceptance of all of the new ministry's legislation and nominations for office, and the reform of the Civil List by parliamentary legislation. In turn, Rockingham's death from influenza on 1 July 1782, at the age of only fifty-two, soon led George to turn to William, 2nd Earl of Shelburne, a former protégé of Chatham. Shelburne's hostility to party was a theme that linked him to George, and in opposition to the view of prominent Rockinghamites, notably Charles James Fox, Shelburne defended the king's right to choose his ministers. However, Shelburne was outmanoeuvred in February 1783 and replaced in April by a ministry headed by Charles James Fox and North, which was a combination unwelcome to George. He personally disliked Fox, the libertine friend of his eldest son, blaming him for leading the prince astray, and seeing him as a threat to the role of the Crown. Fox was the antithesis of what George valued.

George tried to persuade William Pitt the Younger, the Chancellor of the Exchequer and the second son of Chatham, to save him from the choice, but Pitt felt he lacked sufficient support in the Commons. A disappointed George wrote to Pitt:

I am much hurt to find you are determined to decline at an hour when those who have any regard for the constitution as established by law ought to stand forth against the most daring and unprincipled faction that the annals of this kingdom ever produced.[11]

There was considerable force in North's argument for the need for George to respond to circumstances, but the formation of the Fox-North ministry demoralized George, and his habitual self-righteousness brought him no solace. Having revised, but not pursued, his abdication declaration, and probed possibilities as he sought to resist the formation of the new ministry, George now conspicuously failed to show it support. Adopting a grudging tone and sense of acting out of necessity, he made no real attempt to ease differences, still less to be gracious. Elizabeth, Duchess of Manchester, wife of a supporter of the new ministry, reported from court that the king's 'looks and manner strongly mark his dislike to all his present Court – he certainly is endeavouring to work a change as soon as he can.'[12]

Meanwhile, although George shared Shelburne's hopes of benefits from trade with an independent America,[13] the peace settlement, the Treaties of Versailles of 3 September 1783, appeared to be a fundamental weakening of the empire. This response was linked to a widespread sense of Britain as a decayed power, one that encouraged interest in Edward Gibbon's *Decline and Fall of the Roman Empire* (1776–88). The final resolution of the political crisis created by George's unwillingness to accept the coalition, the formation of an eventually stable and successful ministry under Pitt, was far from inevitable.

George's sense of order was challenged not only by politics, but also by his family. Whereas the difficulties he had encountered with his siblings had made George more acutely concerned about his children, the outcome was no happier, and, as their numerous children grew to adulthood, a conflict arose between George and Charlotte's sense of propriety and the dissolute life adopted by most of their brood of boys. In 1780, George had urged Frederick, Duke of York to read the Bible every morning and evening, not least because it provided the opportunity for self-examination.[14] The members of the younger generation were especially loath to accept the king and queen's views on marriage and choice of marriage partners, and entered into liaisons which, while often stable and personally fulfilling, hardly lived up to the increasingly respectable, almost prudish, image that George wished to promote. The alienation between the generations was represented most strikingly in the endless disputes between George and the Prince of Wales. One scandal succeeded another. In 1781, George had to pay £5,000 to buy back the love letters that the prince had written his mistress, Mary Robinson, a prominent actress whom he had seen playing Perdita. Irrespective of the problem of the heir, the need for establishments for his sons was a financial strain for George.

These were difficult years for George in other ways. He had had no experience of miscarriages or stillborn infants to prepare him for the grief when the first of his children died. Born in 1780, Alfred died in 1782, followed in 1783

by Octavius, who had been born in 1779. God was certainly
testing George in his family as well as his reign. George
was a very domestic monarch, which was an outcome of
his character and interests. Indeed, the fluidity of uncon-
strained public socializing clearly worried the king, which
differentiated him from his sons. His hostility to mas-
querades was indicative of his sustained preference for
integrity over artificiality and performance. This critique
of affectation was both an aesthetic and a moral choice, and
his increased dislike of London and favour for the country
was another aspect of it. George also thought early nights
a good idea, and rose early. A dislike of show, and a concern
to avoid the consequences of overeating and drunkenness,
contributed, alongside his shyness and parsimony, to a
simple lifestyle. This way of life, which accorded with the
strengthening of the ideals of privacy and family life in the
French and Habsburg courts, in addition to his interest in
and pursuit of farming, was to lead to the king being
known as 'Farmer George', with its suggestion of ordinar-
iness as well as patriotism.

The court struck observers as pleasantly domestic or dull,
and certainly the opposite of grand. George generally wore
simple clothes, including on his birthday, but wore new
clothes for Charlotte's. In the midst of frequently splendid
entertainment he was cautious in what he ate and drank,
trying not to eat sugar and drinking little alcohol, and was
a model of slimness compared with his eldest son. His attitude to sugar was based on health and not the role of
slaves. Preferring family meals to banquets, and avoiding
grandness, both in what he ate and in how he was served,

George cut down what he consumed in the 1790s in response to the domestic crisis caused by poor harvests. Informality was also seen in George moving among his subjects without guards or servants, or with very few. He had a sense of humour and liked to joke, even if his jokes showed affability rather than wit. At Cheltenham he told the pumper at the spa, Hannah Forty: 'Mrs Forty, you and your husband together make eighty.'[15]

The values of the court were very different to a world of sexual intrigue. Indeed, somewhat fancifully, a critical French observer reported in 1763 that the court resembled an affluent bourgeois household with pleasures constrained by matrimony.[16] Well aware that 'little attentions often do good',[17] George made a practice of speaking to all who attended his levees, which brought him in touch with most of the social elite and, indeed, with many individuals whom he did not know or did not know well. This was a strain for George and for those he met as, under court etiquette, George had to speak first, and courtesy required him to press on if those he met were too nervous to say anything, or if they responded with only a few words. A shy child, George learned to speak in public and to put others at their ease, and those who met the king frequently commented on how agreeable he was, and how much knowledge he showed of individuals and their connections, a characteristic shared with George VI. He was not rude like George II, and was far less waspish than Frederick the Great.

George certainly showed an ease in his contact with people of all ranks that reflected a certainty of position and purpose, and a belief that dignity did not necessarily

lie in social distinction. For him, Christian notions of
benevolence and human sympathy cut across those of hier-
archy. Nevertheless, George was head of society, as his
socializing made clear, while his activities on court days
included the presentations of the young when they came of
age, and of brides and bridegrooms to be, which overlapped
with more official aspects of the recognition of merit, particularly nominations to peerages, investitures and the
kissing of the king's hand by the newly appointed. George
also took an interest in issues of etiquette that arose in
high society, and his role as the fount of honour ensured
that men and women of rank could expect a private audience if they sought one, providing them with the opportunity
to press for patronage.

Ironically, these were the years in which George nearly
found lasting fame of a very different type. On 13 March
1781, William Herschel, Hanoverian-born but British-
settled, discovered Uranus, the first planet to be found since
antiquity and the first that could not be seen by the naked
eye. In honour of the king, Herschel named it the 'Geor-
gium Sidus', a reference to Virgil's *Georgics* that claimed
immortality for George. The following year George met
Herschel, who subsequently exhibited his telescope before
him and became a pensioner of the Crown. Like George's
support for Captain Cook, this was patronage that was of
lasting importance; but at the time he was more absorbed
by the crises of the moment, notably in America.

5
Crisis Overcome

The 1780s were far more challenging for George than the 1770s had been. They brought defeat in America, the crisis of a ministry he did not want, unprecedented health issues with a matching constitutional furore, and the disturbing example of revolution in France. Yet they also saw repeated triumph, most dramatically on 23 April 1789 at St Paul's Cathedral with the service of thanksgiving for his recovery from illness: assessing the numbers that saw him enter and leave Beijing in 1793, George, 1st Earl Macartney, reckoned that the numbers in London were larger. The service at St Paul's was mirrored across the country.

The early years of the decade were more troubled. George had acted in December 1783 against the Fox-North ministry when it backed an East India Bill that he correctly saw as a grab for ministerial power and patronage. The role of the Crown as a bulwark against over-mighty ministers seemed a reality when, in a key show of authority and power, George authorized the comment that any peer voting for the bill would be considered a personal enemy, and refused the ministerial request for permission to disavow the message. Defeated in the Lords on 17 December, the coalition ministry did not resign, so George, pushing the issue further, dismissed it on the 18th, asking Pitt to form a new one. Faced, however, by the continuing unity of the coalition and the collective resignation of many office holders unwilling to serve under Pitt, George saw himself as 'on the edge of a precipice' and hinted again at abdication.[1] Commons defeats in January 1784 led Pitt, who, even with George's help, could not command a parliamentary majority, to think of resigning, and George to reiterate his willingness to abdicate, although declaring his determination to fight on against what he regarded as disorder. The perseverance, stubbornness and inflexibility seen in his handling of America was again evident. By 13 February, the king felt able to comment on

the present strange phenomenon, a majority not exceeding 30 in the House of Commons thinking that justifies stopping the necessary supplies when the House of Lords by a majority of near two to one and at least that of the People at large approve of my conduct and see as I do that not less is meant than to render the Crown and the Lords perfect ciphers; but it will be seen that I will never submit.[2]

The crisis crystallized the ambiguities of the political system, as the deceptive neatness of the formula of parliamentary monarchy does not adequately note the room for disagreement over what it meant in practice in terms of the choice of ministers. To George, executive power was clearly vested in the Crown, and Commons majorities against him in early 1784 only stiffened his determination to persist. Pertinacity was in George's eyes a legitimist creed designed to protect rights (not only his own), and not an aggressive one born of an interest in extending power, a view that linked his opinions in the 1750s to those thereafter. Meanwhile, hanging on helped George and the new ministry to benefit from a swelling tide in popular opinion, shown in a large number of addresses from counties and boroughs, with over 50,000 signatures in total, in favour of the free exercise of the royal prerogative in choosing ministers. These addresses were also a testimony to the potential popularity of the monarchy. In March 1784, Parliament was dissolved and the ministry then did very well in the elections held from 30 March to 10 May. At a meeting of the Yorkshire freeholders, Henry, 2nd Earl Fauconberg, Lord Lieutenant of the North Riding of Yorkshire and George's host at Cheltenham in 1806, taking the pro-governmental stance, asked, 'Is George III or Charles James Fox to reign?' There was a widespread perception of George as a morally respectable Englishman opposed to a bunch of mostly dissolute, power-grabbing aristocrats. George helped finance the ministry's election fund and obtained daily reports on the course of the election, with his interest extending to individual constituencies and candidates.

The overall results – the ministry enjoyed a solid Commons majority – greatly cheered the king and encouraged him to feel that his resolve had not only been vindicated but had helped save the country.[3] The results reflected widespread support for George as the guarantor of stability and continuity, a position very different from two decades or even one year earlier. The royal prerogative, indeed, had become popular, and a caricature, 'The Royal Hercules

Destroying the Dragon Python', published on 24 April 1784, showed George wrestling against a dragon with the heads of the major opposition leaders. The notion of a Patriot King above faction seemed fulfilled, and thereafter the Pitt ministry, which was not a 'party ministry', enjoyed a solid position until the Regency Crisis blew up in late 1788.

There was a renewed burst of popularity for the king when he survived an attempt to kill him in the street outside St James's Palace on 2 August 1786: Margaret Nicholson, his would-be assassin, was mentally ill and convinced that she had a claim to the throne. George was not injured by Nicholson's dessert knife, and instead was solicitous about his assailant: 'the poor creature is mad; do not hurt her, she has not hurt me.' He referred later that month to 'the interposition of Providence in the late attempt on my life by a poor insane woman'.[4]

Despite an irritability that may have been a symptom of poor health, George had matured to become a practised politician. His conscientious nature shines through his copious, well-written correspondence; a conscientiousness that expressed George's conception of service, and his understanding of his position as the pivot of an inclusive civil politics. Although very aggrieved if his goodwill was not reciprocated, George felt that the monarch could reach out, beyond the antipathy and factional self-interest of politicians, to a wider, responsible and responsive public opinion. In practice party politics was as polarized as ever, and for George support for Pitt was a condition of keeping Fox out. Nevertheless, in the mid 1780s George had played a major role in ensuring the creation of a political world that worked for him. Once Crown-elite consensus had been restored – at least in so far as was measured by the crucial criterion, the king's ability to co-operate with a ministry enjoying the support of Parliament – Britain was essentially politically stable. Thanks to the signs of widespread support for the royal position in 1784, George's understanding of his fundamental constitutional role was married to an awareness of the popular resonance of the Crown. He used royal proclamations to galvanize public opinion on a range of issues, including one in 1787 'for the Encouragement of Piety and Virtue', not least through the suppression of 'all loose and licentious prints, books, and publications', against vice and immorality.

Moreover, George had close links with the clergy. Richard Hurd, Bishop of Lichfield, a cleric favoured by George, who appointed him preceptor (tutor) to his two eldest sons, had preached a sermon before the House of Lords in December 1776, presenting the rebellion as divine punishment for the sins of the British people. In 1781, George translated Hurd to Worcester and, in 1783, unsuccessfully urged him to accept Canterbury. George, whose links with the clergy were closer than those of his two predecessors, was to visit Hurd at his country seat in 1788, and in 1805 gave him a collection of books.

From 1784, Pitt dominated parliamentary politics for over two decades, serving as First Lord of the Treasury from December 1783 until 1801, and then again from 1804 until his death in 1806. Pitt's prudent fiscal management helped stabilize government, but he and George disagreed over reform: Pitt was willing in 1785 to support change to the franchise (right to vote), but George was opposed and the measure failed. Nevertheless, the two agreed on most issues, and the support of independent, non-party MPs underlined the significance of royal backing for the ministry, as most independents tended to look to the Crown.

A new style of monarchy was on display during George's travels in 1788, when he took great pains to cultivate popularity. On his visit with Charlotte to the Earl of Coventry's seat at Croome, he and his company were received 'amidst the acclamations of some thousands of all ranks', and walked for over two hours in the grounds, including the dairy and plantations, 'gratifying their own and the curiosity of the numerous spectators, whose plaudits they received with pleasure, and returned to repeated salutes', while:

> After dinner, the royal guests, desirous of satisfying as much as in their power, the wish they had excited, appeared at the windows, where they continued for some time, expressing by their looks and gestures the happiness they experienced in the evident and almost incessant marks of loyalty and affections shown them, by thousands of their surrounding subjects; in fact, the joy of the sovereign, his family, and his people, seemed totally reciprocal.[5]

The impact of such events was increased by their extensive coverage in the press, which brought further publicity to reports of royal gentility and popularity. The article just quoted also reported that the king was delighted 'with the respectable and becoming demeanour of those of inferior rank'.

The extent to which George's serious illness in 1788–9 contributed to a major political crisis was strong evidence of his continued political, constitutional and symbolic importance, for his symptoms of insanity precipitated the Regency Crisis. George's health had generally been good, but, in late October 1788, he began to talk rapidly and uncontrollably, becoming delirious in early November. At the time of the attack George was fifty, and the auguries for a long life were not good, as his father had died at the age of forty-four, and of George's eight siblings, six died before the age of fifty. The alternation of apparent madness with intervals of lucidity, of paroxysms of rage with hours of calm, proved particularly disconcerting, and not only to others, for, when lucid, George was aware of his situation.

It was clear that if there was to be a regency, George, Prince of Wales, now of age, would be regent. The ministry would therefore change, as the prince was close, politically and personally, to Fox. The extent of his likely powers as regent, however, was unclear, and the political interest and inherent drama of the occasion attracted intense public interest. The conduct of the prince and of the Whigs, who were eager for power and hopeful of George's death or continued madness, aroused much criticism, which in turn greatly encouraged sympathy for George.

The king's doctors disagreed as to whether he was likely to recover, until a new doctor, Francis Willis, who declared that George would recover, came to the fore. His methods rested on enforced calm, including the use of a gag, a straitjacket and a restraining chair, which were designed to end the over-excitement that he believed caused madness, and the majesty of monarchy was ignored as George was bullied and coerced. Recovery took time and led to much discussion of medical options; the cricket-loving and womanizing John, 3rd Duke of Dorset, ambassador in Paris, for example, offered a cure that reflects the extent to which in health, as in so much else, the notion of a division between a modernizing enlightened elite and the bulk of the population was, and is, misleading:

> I have always had little or no hopes of the King, I have sent however by this day's courier a remede which they tell me est sure. It is tout simplement the blood of a jack-ass which after passing a clear napkin through it two or three times is given afterwards to the patient to drink. I really hope Willis will try it.[6]

In the meantime, Pitt's attempts to restrict the power of the prince as regent caused controversy, only for George's restoration to health in February 1789 to pre-empt the Whigs. This recovery may only have been partial; but, as far as the public was concerned, it was complete – necessarily so as assumptions about the structure and practice of royal authority required the king's mental and physical health, in both appearance and reality.

George's summer travels after his recovery in 1789 drew even larger crowds than those in 1788, and, alongside growing signs of division in France, this burst of royal popularity generated confidence in the British system, marking a major

change in attitude from the early 1780s. There was a rallying of the social elite and of much opinion around country,
Crown and Church that prefigured the loyalism of the 1790s
in opposition to the French Revolution and the attendant
radicalism in Britain.

In 1789 George first visited Weymouth, where he found
that the sea air and bathing 'certainly agrees'.[7] The king's
trip there gave a new significance to his travels, but also
confirmed his preference for southern England. He went to
Weymouth every year bar three from 1789 to 1805, but
never Liverpool, Manchester, Leeds, York, Newcastle or
Norwich, let alone Hanover, Ireland, Scotland and Wales.
Nor did George travel as widely as Joseph II of Austria or
Gustavus III of Sweden. George's brother-in-law Christian
VII of Denmark toured the north in 1768, proceeding
along the Bridgewater Canal and visiting the industries of
Leeds. George's brother Edward, Duke of York visited York-
shire and Henry, Duke of Cumberland went to Berwick.

Yet George III got to know more about England than
his Hanoverian predecessors. Whereas George I had taken
the waters at Pyrmont in Germany, George III took those
at Cheltenham. He also toured industrial sites, including a
pin manufactory at Gloucester, a carpet works and a china
factory at Worcester, the carpet works at Axminster and
the canals and cloth industry near Stroud. Visiting Worcester in 1788 for the Three Choirs Festival in the cathedral,
George added his own private band to the orchestra. The
festival brought together many of George's concerns, as it
was intended for the relief of the widows and orphans of
the clergy and included a cathedral service, and his visit

provided him with an opportunity to display royal bounty: he left ten guineas for the workmen at the china factory he visited, £50 for the poor of the city (with another £50 from the queen), £200 for the clergy widows and orphans, £300 to liberate debtors, and his pardon to deserving criminals awaiting transportation. The king thus demonstrated concern about the moral and physical welfare of all, which, alongside Christian charity, was important to the extent and motivation of his philanthropy and a counterpart to celebrating the nation's triumphs. George's stance looked forward towards the later emphasis in the royal family on charitable philanthropy.

George was also making himself more generally approachable. Staying with Thomas, 1st Earl of Ailesbury, a friend and also Lord Chamberlain to Charlotte, at Tottenham Park in 1789 on the way back from Weymouth, George not only played cribbage, but drove himself in an open carriage round Savernake Forest, and, more publicly, although in a very controlled fashion, received an address from the mayor and corporation of Marlborough. The reception of such addresses, for example from Worcester in 1788 and from Devizes, Exeter and Plympton in 1789, was an important aspect of George's public politics, with loyalty and graciousness displayed in an interactive pageant, as they also were in Southampton in 1801 and 1804. On their visit to Oxford in 1786, the royal party received addresses from the city and the university, George conferring a knighthood on the senior alderman of the city.

In both Britain and America, rural pursuits were in part a matter of social expression: a proclamation of virtuous activity and appropriate status in the face of the dissolving prospects of the social fluidity represented by new wealth. Alongside sustaining and demonstrating his health, this factor may have played a role for George, but personal preferences were key to his increased favour for Windsor from the 1770s. On his estate there, George's much-reported personal supervision of his tenants was seen as displaying both public and private functions, and helped in the presentation of the human side of the monarch, as with James Gillray's engraving 'Affability' (1795), which depicted George, shown, as so often, as somewhat choleric and inflamed, talking to a surprised rustic. Especially from the 1780s, George was interested in farming, and, in order to permit its pursuit in the Home Park at Windsor, the deer stocked there were moved to the Great Park. George became well known for his agricultural concerns, which bridged patriotism and philanthropy. Farm animals were one of his particular enthusiasms, and in 1804 the 'objects and scenes of the king's favourite amusements and habitual occupations' were described as 'his parks, farming, plantings and building'.[8] George read the *Annals of Agriculture*, toured farms on his estate and investigated agricultural practices when he visited country houses.

George was an active hunter, and keen to protect his interest: when, in 1782, the ministry moved to abolish a whole tranche of household offices, George preserved that of Master of the Buckhounds. References to his frequent hunting occur in George's correspondence and Charlotte's diary. Hunting was also a form of sociability and offered exercise. Windsor's attraction owed much to its access to good

hunting country, for, like much of the social elite, the king
rode frequently, often after breakfast, and was interested
in horses. Indeed, riding was both part of his ordinary routine and a holiday activity. The amount of time that George
devoted to these pursuits is not always readily apparent in
his correspondence, much of which was devoted to governmental business; nor does the correspondence indicate the
people with whom George spent his time. Newspaper
reports provided a useful corrective, as they frequently
noted royal activity. Thus, the *Courier* reported on 14
January 1801:

> His Majesty yesterday morning, attended by Lords Cathcart
> and Walsingham, and Colonel Cartwright, rode to Ascot-
> heath, where a deer was turned out for the day's diversion.
> The King was met by Earl Sandwich, Sir Henry Gott and
> son, Sir John Lade, Mr Freemantle, and a number of gentle-
> men sportsmen.

George made hunting at Windsor easier by appointing
friends and those he could trust to positions there. His uncle
Cumberland, and then his brother Cumberland, were Ran-
gers of Windsor Park; while William Harcourt, later 3rd
Earl Harcourt, was deputy Ranger, as well as a groom of
the bedchamber and deputy Lieutenant of Windsor Castle.
Francis, 2nd Marquis of Hertford, who was Master of the
Horse from 1804 to 1806, had been Cofferer of the House-
hold in 1780–82; James, Lord Brudenell, from 1790 5th
Earl of Cardigan, who had been Master of the Robes to
George as prince, then as king, from 1758 instead became

Constable of Windsor Castle in 1791, holding the position until he died in 1811. George's longevity meant that generations from the same families served him as courtiers and office holders, creating powerful mutual obligations.

George's interest in riding did not preclude walking, and he particularly enjoyed visiting gardens on foot, frequently strolling round those at Kew and Richmond. As natural sights, such as trees in spring bloom, provided the king with evidence of the 'goodness of Divine Providence', it is not surprising that he relished being outdoors.[9] George was a strider, not a stroller, and he pushed himself forward, his walking in part reflecting the nervous intensity seen in much of his conversation. Walking a lot helped keep the king fit, although it was another of the many activities that left few traces in his correspondence.

Propriety was a key term of praise from the king, who expected decorum in both public and private life. His correspondence makes it clear that he favoured those whose demeanour suggested seriousness and whose behaviour was appropriate. This attitude also, however, led to a lack of tolerance for others, most obviously John Wilkes, Charles James Fox and George, Prince of Wales, all of whom were seen (not unfairly) as irresponsible rakes with dangerous political views. The bleaker side of his concern with duty, uprightness and decorum was shown in George's support for the moral strictures and penalties of society, although in terms of the ones he supported he was very much a figure of his time. Thus, homosexual acts in the navy earned his condemnation as 'a most detestable and unnatural crime'.[10] More generally, George's correspondence upholding the execution or pardoning of convicted felons reveals him as conscientious and firm. In these, as in other attitudes (for example, he was critical of suicides), George was not out of line with a dominant ethos that treated religion, conduct and morality not as private activities outside the ken of public supervision, but as matters of concern and control.

The wayward behaviour of his brothers and sons was, for George, a matter of far more than inappropriate conduct and royal embarrassment. The firm attitude to parenthood that reflected an emphasis on duty and responsibilities that characterized George and Charlotte's own youth did not have the desired effect. As adults, the sons did not suffer the constraints their sisters encountered, but in earlier days the king's love for them was expressed in a carefully planned emphasis on dutiful conduct and exemplary education, only for the response to be similar to that of many American colonists: royal good intentions did not suffice, and when, in his eyes, the king sought to reduce passion to order he was frequently defeated. He expected his sons to cultivate a strip on a model farm he had devised, an activity they did not relish. Frederick, Duke of York was a favourite of the king, who tried to ensure not only an exemplary upbringing but also continuing supervision; yet George had to face his son's losses of large sums in gambling and racing. Gambling, a fashionable activity in the aristocratic salons of London, was a pastime that underscored the difference between parents and sons, for, to the princes, gambling provided and symbolized excitement and style.

The royal family was conspicuously short of the dutiful love George had sought to ensure. He bears some of the responsibility because of his failure to understand his siblings and children, and to help create appropriate roles for them. The six princesses had pleasant early years and did not experience the firm discipline meted out to their brothers, with whom they spent a fair amount of time. This warm family background lasted until George's illness in 1788–9, although, as the princes grew older and lived away, the contrast between the life of the girls and the independence of their brothers became more apparent and more trying to the girls, who complained about living, under their mother's unwelcome dominance, in a 'Nunnery', where they were kept under supervision and constantly chaperoned. Charlotte, who regularly read sermons to them, wanted the girls to stay close to her, and also feared that any discussion of their marriage would threaten George's mental stability, as he was known to be unsettled about the idea. This meant that they could not preside over their own households, and Charlotte, the eldest, who married the hereditary prince of Württemberg in 1797, was the sole daughter to marry before the Regency. George had been opposed because he thought the prince unpleasant, but the marriage was to be reasonably happy. As was to be expected in an age when members of ruling families travelled little, George never again saw his daughter, who shared his agricultural and architectural interests. Faced with this parental attitude, three of the daughters had secret marriages, two of them bearing children.

George was more indulgent to his daughter-in-law (and niece) Caroline of Brunswick, wife of George, Prince of Wales, to her mother in exile and to her daughter, his granddaughter, Charlotte. If the king's legacy was an uncomfortable one as far as his heir was concerned, that was principally due to his encouragement of his son's disastrous marriage. Unhappily for George, one aspect of the failure was that this most family-conscious of monarchs had only one legitimate grandchild before his final loss of sanity. In 'Grandpappa in his Glory!!!', a caricature of 1796, James Gillray depicted him as a doting figure, happily feeding Charlotte as she sat on his knee. George was keen to maintain close relations with his granddaughter, then, despite his fifteen children, his sole grandchild and his likely successor or successor bar one, and his loss of sanity at least spared him the knowledge that Charlotte died in childbirth in November 1817; the baby, who would have been George's first great-grandchild, was not saved. George never saw the granddaughter who was eventually to succeed him, Victoria, born in May 1819 to his fourth son, Edward, Duke of Kent.

By the end of the 1780s, George was the beneficiary of a popularity that stemmed from the specific events of 1783–4 and his recent illness, but also from a more general attention, in the developing moral climate of the period, to the royal family. A concern with probity and honourable conduct could not but highlight the contrast between George and his eldest son, as well as the supporting contrast between Pitt and Fox. George did not change his opinions, but benefited from a widely grounded shift in social sensibility, acceptable behaviour and political attitudes. As a young man George had received his political education in a context in which patriotism, integrity and honour were linked, but the social resonance of order was less focused on the personality of the monarch, while the moralizing religious dimension, which was to be present towards the end of the century as Evangelical piety became more significant in British culture, was less pronounced. George gained in confidence, purpose and reputation from the shift, symbolizing a much-desired stability at a time of rapid, and to many disconcerting, social change, and in the aftermath of a major and humiliating national crisis.

George's support for England as a Church state was affirmed in the late 1780s when attempts were made to repeal the Test and Corporation Acts of 1673 and 1661 respectively. These acts obliged office holders under the Crown both to take Oaths of Allegiance and Supremacy that accepted the position of the Crown as Supreme Governor of the Church of England, and to receive Communion in the Church of England. Moves, backed by the opposition Whigs, to repeal the acts were defeated in 1787, 1789 and 1790, which helped ensure a continued role for Anglicanism in national identity. As Dissenters were outside the established Church they suffered civic disabilities, saw themselves as second-class figures and gravitated towards more radical political positions. George's view of a threat to the constitution was more generally shared. In 1790, the Reverend Thomas Brand wrote to a fellow Anglican cleric, Thomas Wharton, rejoicing in:

the defeat of the Dissenters. Their success would have opened a door to every vile set of petitions which ambitious demagogues and disaffected spirits could have invented and the constitution must have been completely destroyed if the votes of Parliament could have been thus influenced by associations from without.[11]

George had been able to recover from the loss of America and struck an appropriate note of wise and honest courtesy when he received John Adams on 1 June 1785 as the first American Minister to the Court of St James's. Adams recorded George as saying:

> I have done nothing in the late contest but what I thought myself indispensably bound to do, by the duty which I owed to my people ... I was the last to consent to the separation; but the separation having been made, and having become inevitable, I have always said, as I say now, that I would be the first to meet the friendship of the United States as an independent power ... let the circumstances of language, religion, and blood have their natural and full effect.

George, who, Adams noted, was 'much affected and answered me with more tremor than I had spoken with', was revealed as informed, relaxed and quick-witted. With 'an air of familiarity, and smiling, or rather laughing', he astutely teased Adams by saying, 'there is an opinion among some people that you are not the most attached of all your countrymen to the manners of France,' and it was Adams, not George, who was wrong-footed and stood more on his dignity. 'Surprised' and 'embarrassed', he responded that he had 'no attachment but to my own country', which George, 'as quick as lightning', courteously trumped, saying, 'an honest man will never have any other,' a reflection that joined two of the king's main values, patriotism and civility,[12] and he emerged from the exchange as the gentleman he assuredly was.

George was also a symbol for empire, not least with the singing of 'God Save the King' across the face of the world. At Botany Bay in 1789, the convicts staged George Farquhar's classic comedy *The Recruiting Officer* in celebration of the king's birthday. Similar themes echoed in Britain. For 22 August 1791, the audience at Birmingham's New Street Theatre was offered:

> A pantomime exhibition called Botany Bay; or, A Trip to Port Jackson, with entire new scenery, painted for the occasion . . . in which will be introduced a picturesque view of the coast of New South Wales, arrival of the Grand Fleet, landing, reception, and employment of the convicts. To conclude with the ceremony of planting the British flag, on taking possession of a new discovered island, with a dance by the convicts, and the grand chorus of 'God Save the King'.

Moreover, the names of George and Charlotte were attached to British settlements across the world, for example Charlotte, North Carolina and Georgetown (British Guiana), as well as George Street in Sydney. The British presence in Malaysia began in 1786 with the establishment of a base named George Town. As a result, their legacy continues to this day all over the world.

6

In Response to Revolution

Revolution in France dramatized the position of kings, and notably so with the guillotining of Louis XVI in the Place de la Révolution in Paris on 21 January 1793. George's increasingly hostile position was pushed to the fore as British politicians defined monarchy as a distinctive characteristic deserving of support, which was highlighted by the extent to which, in contrast, radical sentiment in Britain was empowered by the example of revolution, such that republicanism came into wider consideration. On 30 January 1793, Samuel Horsley, Bishop of St David's, protégé of George's favourite Thurlow, and trusted by the king, gave the annual Martyrdom Day sermon in Westminster Abbey before the House of Lords. Marking the anniversary of the execution of Charles I, 30 January had often served in the first third of the century to articulate crypto-Jacobite critiques of the legitimacy of Hanoverian rule and had often been a focus for discontent and riots. In 1793, in contrast, the day affirmed not the Stuart house but the institution of monarchy itself. Delivering a powerful attack on political speculation and revolutionary theory in which he stressed royal authority, Horsley presented the constitution as the product and safeguard of a 'legal contract' between Crown and people, with the obedience of the latter a religious duty. The congregation rose to its feet in approval.

The radical critique and challenge varied greatly in its intensity during the 1790s. There was a peak in 1792, one that led to a loyalist counter-rallying. George was firmly opposed to radicalism, and keen to be kept informed about its progress. At the same time as the king supported his ministry in pursuing vigorous steps abroad, he expected to do likewise in domestic policy. He was aware that the government was becoming more authoritarian, albeit within an established legal context, and he welcomed this as necessary. However, the attendant harrying of the radical press, while effective, did not end the challenge, as repeated problems in the conduct of the war with revolutionary France that began in 1793, combined with severe economic strains in Britain, led to a strengthening of radicalism in the late 1790s. Particular difficulties were caused by disobedience in the navy in 1797 and rebellion in Ireland in 1798. George showed his inflexible side when he insisted that the death sentences decreed for naval mutineers, who had threatened British naval capability, should be enforced. For most sailors, this mutiny was a mass protest about conditions, especially a failure to raise wages and the operation of the bounty system, rather than an attempt to overthrow the regime. More generally, George's correspondence with George, 2nd Earl Spencer, First Lord of the Admiralty, reveals him as a methodical dispenser of justice, ready to support his officials and keen to see order maintained.

George's close interest in naval issues was a matter not only of correspondence with the First Lord, but also of

1. George, Prince of Wales, aged sixteen, by Jean-Étienne Liotard.

2. George's loving father, Frederick, Prince of Wales, who died when George was twelve, by Godfrey Kneller. 'Poor Fred', as he came to be known, bequeathed many of his noblest thoughts and principles to his son.

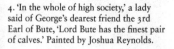

3. George's much abused but guiltless mother, Princess Augusta, by Allan Ramsay. Rumours about her love life meant that she was booed at her funeral, but George knew them to be untrue.

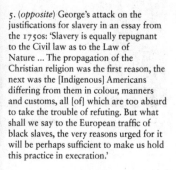

4. 'In the whole of high society,' a lady said of George's dearest friend the 3rd Earl of Bute, 'Lord Bute has the finest pair of calves.' Painted by Joshua Reynolds.

5. (opposite) George's attack on the justifications for slavery in an essay from the 1750s: 'Slavery is equally repugnant to the Civil law as to the Law of Nature ... The propagation of the Christian religion was the first reason, the next was the [Indigenous] Americans differing from them in colour, manners and customs, all [of] which are too absurd to take the trouble of refuting. But what shall we say to the European traffic of black slaves, the very reasons urged for it will be perhaps sufficient to make us hold this practice in execration.'

Slavery is equaly repugnant to the Civil Laws as to the Law of Nature. a Slave is no Member of Society, he cannot therefore be restrain'd by Laws in what has no interest, from attempting to procure liberty by flight; the legal authority of the Master only can prevent him.

The pretexts used by the Spaniards for enslaving the New World were extremely curious; the propagation of the Christian Religion was the first reason, the next was the Americans differing from them in colour, manners & Customs, all which are too absurd to take the trouble of relating;

But what shall we say to the European Traffic of Black Slaves, the very reasons urg'd for it will be perhaps sufficient to make us hold this practice in execration.

6. George Grenville thought similarly to the King on a wide range of issues, including over the taxation of the North American colonies, but their personalities clashed.

7. William Pitt the Elder, the hero of the Seven Years War, was a recluse for most of his last premiership – due to depression brought on by chronic gout, for which his doctor prescribed alcohol as a cure.

8. The 3rd Duke of Grafton failed to heed the warning signals from the American colonies.

9. The Marquess of Rockingham repealed Grenville's hated Stamp Tax, but too late.

10. George, Queen Charlotte and their six eldest children. George, Prince of Wales, and Frederick, Duke of York, stand beside their father; William, Duke of Clarence, holds a cockatoo; Edward, Duke of Kent, plays with a dog. The Queen holds the infant Princess Augusta, while Princess Charlotte stands alongside.

11. George bought Buckingham House for Queen Charlotte in 1762, extensively renovating and adding to it. Fourteen of their fifteen children were born there.

12. The King's Octagonal Library at Buckingham House, where he kept some of his 80,000 books and where he met Samuel Johnson in 1767.

13. George founded the Royal Academy of Arts, and had its original members painted by Zoffany in 1772. Among others in this picture are Giovanni Cipriani, the American-born Benjamin West, Paul and Thomas Sandby, William Chambers and Joshua Reynolds.

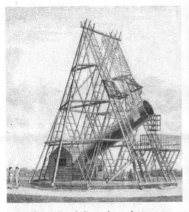

14. William Herschel's 40-foot telescope was built at Slough in 1787 with funds from George III.

15. A silver microscope commissioned by the King from George Adams *c.* 1770.

16. George's design for a neo-classical Corinthian temple at Kew, drawn as an exercise for his tutor William Chambers, *c.* 1759, when he was still Prince of Wales. The numerous compass holes down the centre, across its base and in the centre-left column suggest painstaking work.

17. John Harrison's H5 Chronometer, which enabled longitude to be determined with precision for the first time. George ensured that Harrison was awarded a magnificent £20,000 prize for his invention.

18. Kew Palace, also known as the Dutch House, where George and his brother Prince Edward were educated in 1750s and where their mother the Dowager Princess Augusta lived until her death in 1772 and where Queen Charlotte died in 1819.

19. Thomas Pelham-Holles, 1st Duke of Newcastle, personified the Old Whigs whose power George wanted to reduce.

20. George's uncle, William Augustus, Duke of Cumberland, in 1758. George and his mother wrongly suspected him of plotting a coup against them.

21. Allan Ramsay's Coronation Portrait of 1762. No fewer than 179 copies were made, rendering it the most famous image of the King.

22. On 9 July 1776 the equestrian statue of George III on the Bowling Green in Lower Manhattan was pulled down by a revolutionary crowd. It was turned into 41,000 lead musket balls for the Continental Army.

23–25. (*left*) George Germain, 1st Viscount Sackville, formulated the strategic plan for fighting the war in America, but failed to ensure that it was properly executed; (*centre*) Frederick, Lord North, was a charming and good-natured peacetime prime minister, but a dismal wartime leader; (*right*) John Montagu, 4th Earl of Sandwich, was an able First Lord of the Admiralty but presided over the naval side of the American debacle.

26–30. (*top left*) General Sir Thomas Gage was overwhelmed by events in Boston, Lexington and Concord; (*top right*) General Sir John Burgoyne was outmanoeuvred and forced to surrender his army at Saratoga; (*centre*) General Sir William Howe failed to adhere to the Germain Plan and go to Burgoyne's rescue, but instead took the rebel capital of Philadelphia; (*bottom left*) General Lord Cornwallis occupied an indefensible peninsula at Yorktown and dallied there too long; (*bottom right*) General Sir Henry Clinton took over an impossible position in the final years of the war.

31. General George Washington, an inspired leader, whom George III eventually came to describe as 'the greatest character of the age'. He is here depicted with his enslaved valet and groom William Lee.

32. Thomas Paine, who described George as a 'royal brute' in his bestselling pamphlet *Common Sense* in 1776.

33. John Trumbull's painting of 1818 depicting the five-man drafting committee of the Declaration of Independence presenting their work to the Continental Congress on 28 June 1776. The Declaration's sublime language hid the fact that it was largely wartime propaganda – only two of its twenty-eight charges were true.

34. The great orator, philosopher and polemicist Edmund Burke started his career in opposition to George, but ended it as an enthusiastic ideological ally.

35. Charles Fox's open contempt for George helped to keep him out of high office for all but nineteen months in a political career of almost forty years.

36. The dissolution of Parliament in March 1784 depicted as a thunderbolt hurled by George on Pitt's behalf against Fox, Burke and North.

37. George, Prince of Wales, took friends gleefully to Windsor in November 1788 to witness his father's descent into severe bipolar disorder. Caricaturist Thomas Rowlandson denounces his lack of 'Filial Piety'.

38. Six thousand charity children occupied huge stands at St Paul's Cathedral for the national Service of Thanksgiving for the King's recovery, held on St George's Day in April 1789.

39. A letter from Queen Charlotte to George written the day after he was forcibly removed from Kew Palace in April 1801 reads, 'My dearest King ... Our separation must be and really is equally painful to us both.'

My dearest King & John Willis has made me very
happy by putting into my Hands Your very Affectionate Letter, which contains Your Approbation of
my Conduct which both my Inclination & Duty
led me to fullfill & which will never cease but with
my Life. Our Separation must be & really is
equally painfull to us both & happy as it would
make me & Your Children to come & see You.
The Physicians assure me That such a meeting
ought not to take place at present & therefore
am under the painfull Necessity to deprive
myself of so Satisfactory a pleasure which
would prove a happiness to

Kew
April the 22d
1801

Your truely attached Wife
Charlotte

40. George, Prince of Wales, later George IV, was a mendacious, self-pitying spendthrift with a fine taste in art.

41. Queen Charlotte's hair went white overnight when her husband suffered his second bout of manic depression, as shown by Sir Thomas Lawrence in 1789.

42. In 1786 caricaturist James Gillray depicted the supposed venality of the King and Queen, who are here leaving the Treasury with gold coins pouring out of their pockets and being offered more by a sycophantic Pitt the Younger while the Prince of Wales is bailed out by Philippe, Duc d'Orléans.

43. William Pitt addressing the House of Commons in 1793; Charles Fox can be seen wearing a hat by the Speaker's chair, seated sixth from the right.

44. George III in military uniform during the Napoleonic Wars, painted by William Beechey in 1799.

The Thieves detected at last or a Wonderful discovery at the Windsor Farm!!

45. A satirical print of the King and Queen dressed as a farmer and his wife watching in astonishment as two geese suck a cow's udder. The King's interest in progressive agriculture, on which he wrote well-informed articles for journals, earned him the nickname 'Farmer George'.

The REPUBLICAN-ATTACK

46. Gillray's satirical depiction of the attack on George's coach on his way to open Parliament on 29 October 1795. Here it is Charles Fox, Richard Sheridan and the radical Whigs who make up the mob stoning the coach.

47. The greatest statesman and orator of the era and saviour of his country: William Pitt the Younger. His relationship with George was mutually supportive and respectful but never intimate.

48. The King on holiday at Weymouth in 1797, depicted by James Gillray. He visited fourteen times between 1789 and 1805.

49. George's bathing machine at Weymouth continued in use until 1916. A string quartet played from an adjoining machine as the King went swimming.

50. George taking the waters at Cheltenham, thought to be the last likeness drawn of him from life.

51. James Gillray contrasting George as the King of Brobdingnag and Napoleon as Gulliver, in 1803. When George describes Napoleon as 'one of the most pernicious little odious reptiles that nature ever suffered to crawl upon the surface of the earth', he was not, from the British perspective, being satirical.

52. Gillray depicting George's dismissal of Lord Grenville's 'Broad-Bottomed' ministry in 1807 over the issue of Catholic emancipation, which George believed contradicted his Coronation Oath.

53. William Grenville was the last Whig Prime Minister for over twenty years.

54. The 3rd Duke of Portland moved ideologically towards George during his long career in politics.

55. Spencer Perceval, the last Prime Minister George appointed, was assassinated in 1812.

56. Robert Jenkinson, 2nd Earl of Liverpool, became the longest-serving Prime Minister in British history.

57. The Royal Family promenading on the North Terrace of Windsor Castle, in 1783.

58. Massive nationwide celebrations for the King's Golden Jubilee on 25 October 1809 took place days before George succumbed to his final, decade-long bout of lunacy.

59. Deaf, blind, suffering from manic depression and latterly also senility, and unvisited by his family, the King lived at Windsor for ten long years before his death.

corresponding with, and meeting, individual admirals, for example Richard, 1st Earl Howe in 1795. He visited the victorious fleets when they returned from the Glorious First of June in 1794 and Camperdown in 1797 and, also in 1797, took the leading role in the Naval Thanksgiving held in St Paul's Cathedral, after he had processed in state through the thronged streets of London. The king's reception was better than that of Pitt.

The domestic radicalism that accompanied the French Revolution led to an upsurge in republicanism, with publications such as Richard Lee's pamphlet *The Death of Despotism, and the Doom of Tyrants* (1795). The execution of Louis XVI helped focus the interest of British radicals on the position of the king, although some of the plotters were less interested in killing him than in detaining and re-educating him to act as king in a revolutionary democracy; indeed, for many republicans, allegiance and national identity were still manifested in dynastic terms. Yet threats to George's life led to the reconsideration of the law of treason. Although he kept his customary aplomb, he was affected by a mob attack on his carriage en route to the opening of Parliament in 1795 and he was also fired on by James Hadfield at a performance of *The Marriage of Figaro* in Drury Lane Theatre in 1800. An unflinching sense of duty was reflected in his bravery during these episodes, and the king's display of composure won him considerable praise, was widely reported and led to bursts of loyalist sentiment. The Lord Chancellor, John, 1st Earl of Eldon, recorded George as saying to a startled attendant of rank when his coach was apparently shot at in 1795: 'Sit still,

Sir, let us not betray any fear of what may happen.' The *Morning Chronicle* on 23 May 1800 reported him saying, 'A man on such an occasion should immediately feel what is his duty.' In 1802, Edward Despard plotted a coup in which George was to be killed on his way to open Parliament. George followed the trial with interest and, when Despard refused to attend chapel or receive the Sacrament after he was condemned to death, reflected: 'It is melancholy that a man should appear so void of religion at so awful a moment.'[1] Such attempts, however, were unusual.

George found his role anew as a war monarch, and the reviews of troops seen in the War of American Independence were repeated from 1792. Such opportunities satisfied George's desire to do something active, associated him with the war effort and created personal links, transient, but remembered, with large numbers; links frequently by word and, at least, by sight. On his holiday in Weymouth in 1794, George saw the Dorset Yeomanry exercise and he reviewed the Buckinghamshire Militia. Once returned to Windsor, he inspected the Surrey Yeomanry at Epsom on 24 October, and the Prince of Wales's Regiment of Light Dragoons on Ashford Common on 7 November, while in 1804 the presence at Weymouth of the heavy cavalry meant that George could wear his Horse Guards uniform. George devoted much time to the details of military honours and promotion, seeking to use both in an exemplary fashion in order to foster morale and professionalism, and his correspondence showed his repeated concerns with these issues. In the 1790s, he increasingly adopted a quasi-military dress code around the so-called 'Windsor Uniform', versions of which his family, courtiers and staff were encouraged to wear.

George was a firm critic of developments within France, and in May 1792, misleadingly but prophetically, claimed that 'from the commencement of the revolution more acts of barbarity have been committed than by the most savage people.'[2] George was not an ultra, however; he was correctly wary of claims about the scale of royalist support in France, and did not press for the restoration of the Bourbons as a crucial war goal, yet, although unenthusiastic about fighting on for them, he came to agree that Jacobinism could not be destroyed 'unless Royalty is re-established'.[3] George wanted France beaten, and, whether Britain experienced victory or defeat in the war, he pressed for resolve in the struggle. In James Gillray's 1793 caricature 'A new Map of England and France. The French Invasion; or John Bull Bombarding the Bum-Boats', in which the French threat is dispersed with excremental force, John Bull was given George's face.

George kept a close eye on military policy and made informed comments. Unlike most of the leading ministers of the period, the king had had experience in directing a war, that of American Independence, although it had not been a successful experience.

King and ministry united in pursuit of victory, but there were tensions. Facing France's military successes from 1794, the ministry, much to George's concern, was more willing than he was to begin negotiations with Paris. George doubted that a lasting peace could be negotiated with an outlaw regime that lacked legitimacy, and he believed that

France had to be defeated before there could be a basis for fruitful negotiations, an attitude that affected his response to talks in 1796 and 1797. In addition, he habitually adopted a moral tone, and feared that seeking peace would weaken Britain accordingly: for George, the issue of negotiations was one in which honour and integrity were aspects of prudence. The failure of negotiations in 1797, which eased tensions with the ministry, left George hopeful that if Britain acted firmly it could win an honourable and lasting peace, helped by factional struggles in Paris and the exhaustion of French resources.

So again in 1799–1800. Initially confident that Napoleon, who had seized power in a 'shameless revolution' on 9–10 November 1799,[4] could not last for long, George was against peace while 'French principles' continued, and until there was a stable government on which reliance could be placed. Disagreeing with Pitt, who was more willing to countenance a peace that he (correctly) thought could not be sustained, George typically saw his view as uniquely principled, not least because he emphasized his consistency: 'My opinion is formed on principle, not on events and therefore is not open to change.'[5]

A more serious dispute arose from Ireland. Anxious that disaffection there should not lead to a fresh rebellion after that supported by an unsuccessful French invasion but suppressed in 1798, the ministry sought 'Catholic Emancipation' in the shape of an end to civil disabilities in office-holding. This was part of a process by which Catholic loyalty had been sought and rewarded. Indeed, George had, conspicuously, stayed with prominent Catholics on his tours during the American War of Independence. However, over Catholic Emancipation he was unwilling to match the government and brought up his Coronation Oath to protect the established Church and the confessional state. In his case, inherent conservatism was linked to a stubborn determination to protect the constitution and the Church of England, and thus the traditional, as well as legal, character of authority and power.

To a great extent George was opposed to a more comprehensive and progressive national mobilization. To strengthen the country, the late 1790s and early 1800s saw the introduction of income tax, the first national census, parliamentary union with Ireland, laws to restrict trade unionism, and increased state mapping by the Ordnance Survey; Catholic Emancipation was an aspect of this modernization and associated in particular with Pitt, who was a reformer by instinct as well as expedience. George provided a different emphasis to Britain under attack: his was not so much an *ancien régime* capable of adaptation as a defence of order and continuity for their own sake. In part, the contrast captures a generational one, with George just old enough to be Pitt's father; but it also reflects the range of British conservatism. At any rate, George was not a British enlightened despot, as Frederick the Great or Joseph II had been, and as Napoleon sought to be. Meanwhile, the king's personal and cultural preferences continued to display his emphasis on continuity. His travels focused on Weymouth and he did not alter his routine there. So also at court, where George's struggle with the Whig aristocracy and his preference for a sober and moral order were realigned with the new politics of the war. The king's position helped ensure that he could not readily be criticized for extravagance and, instead, George's lifestyle was well suited to the symbol of a prudent and public-spirited monarchy. Dedicated to George, John Nichols's *History and Antiquities of the County of Leicester* (1795) appropriately described the king as 'Patron of the Arts and Sciences, and Father of his People'.

George's dispute with Pitt was not to the fore as far as the public was concerned. Instead, the monarchy had become a potent symbol of national identity and continuity in response to the French Revolution. George benefited from the strength not only of loyalism, in the sense of an active opposition to democratic and republican tendencies, but also of loyal adherence to non-partisan principles of constitutional propriety and support for the established order. Opposition criticisms failed to gain political or popular traction. The monarchy played a greater role in political ideology than it had done between 1689 and 1746, when it had been compromised by serious differences over the legitimacy of the dynasty, as well as the contentious nature of constitutional arrangements after 1688. But from the 1790s no such problems limited a stress on the king on the part of conservative elements and this contributed to the stronger conservative ideology of the period.

The distancing of George from the daily processes of government expanded to fight a war of unprecedented difficulty, a distancing that increasingly characterized the Pitt years and also contributed to George's growing popularity. This was particularly so as the ministry gained cohesion around Pitt, not least with the grudging dismissal by George in June 1792 of Thurlow, the Lord Chancellor, the last major 'King's Friend'. Unpopular decisions were now blamed on the ministers, while the Crown demonstrated its largely non-partisan usefulness by standing above parties in defence of the constitution, including the constitutionally established Church, and was thus the guardian of what had become popularly known to its defenders as 'the Protestant consti-tution'. George himself contributed to this positive image, not by making a special effort to change, but by being himself. In addition, a series of gestures underlined his commitment to the country. These included the payment of £20,000 from his Privy Purse to the Voluntary Contri-bution of 1798, and the extension of taxation to the private income of the Crown resulting from the passage of the Crown Private Estates Act of 1800. Yet, alongside this dis-tancing, George continued to take an active interest in government activity, for example that of the navy. His was a rulership both active and symbolic.

7
'Good King George's Glorious Days!'[1]

Napoleon brought a new challenge to George in imagery and practice. Seizing power in a coup in 1799, he became First Consul, promoting himself to Emperor in 1804, which was a rank and a grandeur that George lacked, and his repeated victories challenged George's confidence in Divine Providence. In 1805–7 French armies defeated the forces of Austria, Prussia and Russia, reordering central Europe, going on to conquer much of Spain in 1808 and defeating Austria anew, although not so easily, in 1809. By late 1812, Napoleon's legions had reached Moscow. Meanwhile, European dynasties had been recast, and in 1810 Napoleon's second marriage, to Marie Louise, the daughter of Francis I, Emperor of Austria, demonstrated Napoleon's effective dominance of European royalty.

Yet if in 1742, 1744 and 1782 the British monarchy had appeared one of the weakest in Europe, its rulers unable to sustain in office ministers who enjoyed royal confidence – Sir Robert Walpole, John, Lord Carteret and North respectively – by 1810 it was the strongest in Europe other than the Romanov regime in Russia and Napoleon's monarchical dictatorship, which lacked comparable legitimacy.

In contrast with the stance of George V towards the Romanovs of Russia once they were overthrown in 1917, other European rulers, such as Louis XVIII, the Kings of Naples, Portugal and Sardinia and William V of Orange (first cousin of George), took shelter in Britain, or sought protection behind British forces, especially the navy, as in the cases of Ferdinand IV of Naples in Sicily, Victor Emmanuel I, ruler of Savoy-Piedmont, who took refuge in Sardinia, and John VI of Portugal in Brazil.

In this survival and resistance, George might appear to be somewhat inconsequential. He had survived bouts of ill-health in 1801 and 1804, but his vigour was fading and his eyesight going; indeed, he was in some respects becoming yesterday's man. His importance, however, was pushed to the fore as a consequence of the revival in the 1800s of ministerial instability as well as the importance of royal resolve. In his sixties, George was still playing a central role, not least his part in the downfall of Pitt, the most powerful prime minister of his reign, in 1801. George's opposition to Catholic Emancipation was crucial in this episode. The establishment of a new ministry in 1801 gave him the opportunity to take a more active part in government, which was necessary if a stable ministry was to be created.

George remained convinced that politics was a struggle of good versus evil, one in which Providence played a key role, but this did not provide an easy basis for policy and politics. Concerned to do the proper thing, George sought to accommodate change to accustomed order, and as a consequence he was opposed to what he saw as unnecessary governmental innovation. At the same time, George was a hard-working monarch, and his oversight of government enabled him to make qualitative statements about the conduct of business, as well as to respond to the management of individuals.

The style of monarchy remained public magnificence, where necessary, and private modesty, the latter in accordance with 'middle-class' mores and cultural aspirations, and also with that part of the aristocracy adhering to Christian and modest standards. Alongside reports of George as an accessible individual, walking, riding and travelling without pomp and state, indeed any protection (especially outside London), came the reporting of court life, which presented a very different resonance. Tone and accessibility did not mean that George's lifestyle was that of the middling orders, for he was head of society in what was very much an aristocratic monarchy, making court routines very important. The splendour of the court, its settings and activities, and yet also George's willingness to be a working ruler, in this case spending time with key ministers, was shown in the report in the *Courier* of 20 January 1801 about the celebration of the queen's birthday held in the ballroom at St James's Palace the previous night:

At a quarter past ten, the King rose, which was the signal for the dancing to conclude . . . Mr Pitt, the Duke of Portland, and the Earl of Chatham, to whom he addressed himself all the evening . . . The King was dressed in scarlet and gold, and wore a great quantity of the richest diamonds, different orders, his star, sword-hilt, button and loop, rings, etc; but above all a Turkish aigrette fastened in his hat, which he held on his arm, exposing the aigrette to full view. In the shape of a hand, it was composed of a vast number of the finest diamonds ever beheld, which attracted and fixed the attention of the whole room. Behind it was a heron's feather, worth at least £500. The King was in excellent spirits, laughed much, and chatted all the time with his ministers.

In February 1801, at a time of government crisis over the future of the Pitt ministry, George suddenly became very ill, a suggestive link, although there had been other crises without illness. There was nothing to match the traumatic 1788–9 crisis, because of the experience of the earlier episode, and because the 1801 attack lasted less than a month; while the potential repercussions were contained when the Prince of Wales agreed to Pitt's proposal that if George failed to recover, there would be a restricted regency. The 1801 crisis, in which George was affected by the determination of Robert and John Willis, the sons of Francis, to force health on him by detention and restraint, left him weaker and under stress, while his relationship with Charlotte was badly affected. The trip to Weymouth that summer again brought him much-needed relief, notably as a result of gentle exercise, but it was clear that difficult issues caused him problems, and his nervous irritability helped provoke another bout of ill-health in early 1804. In June, Princess Mary advised her father's doctors to suggest things 'in such a way that the King imagines the first thought was his own', to let him voice his grievances, both 'real and imaginary', and to 'keep everything in order without ever having a squabble'.[2] Ministers anxiously considered the implications of George's health for the monarchy. Again, Weymouth helped bring recovery. Yet a separate issue, poor eyesight, became serious in 1805 and greatly affected the legibility of George's writing, while his speech from the throne at the start of the session that year was the last he ever delivered personally to Parliament, and a sense of mortality was driven home in August when William, Duke of Gloucester, his last surviving brother, died.

Christian fortitude continued to offer George solace, and he remained politically important. He could also be flexible, as when he called on Henry Dundas, former Secretary of State for War, after the 1801 Egyptian expedition to admit that he had been wrong to oppose his plan to send a force to contest French control of Egypt. However, there were serious challenges to George's views because it proved impossible to recreate a political and governmental force as impressive as that of Pitt, who was succeeded by Henry Addington at the head of a weak ministry (1801–4). George backed him, not least because he feared that an alternative administration might seek to reintroduce Catholic Emancipation and because he saw Addington, the son of a doctor, as an ordinary man after his own heart and a 'truly beloved friend' whom he could trust.[3] In contrast, while George respected Pitt, he had never really liked him.

Nevertheless, Addington was seen, even by George, to lack leadership for war, which, after a gap following the Treaty of Amiens (25 March 1802), was resumed with France in May 1803. George, who had supported a firm stance towards France during the brief peace, played a major political role in symbolizing opposition to the prospect of invasion. On 26 and 28 October 1803, he reviewed 27,000 volunteers in Hyde Park, in each case in front of an estimated half a million people. George's sons played a role in the war effort, notably York, who was commander-in-chief from 1795 to 1809 and, after a scandal could be overlooked, 1811 to 1827. Although a failed campaign commander in Holland in 1799, York was an effective and impressive administrator, and his care for merit in the army matched his father's for merit in the Church. Despite his naval career, the more limited William, Duke of Clarence, later William IV (r. 1830–37), did not put to sea during the war, but Ernest, Duke of Cumberland served with Hanoverian forces, gaining a justified reputation for bravery, while Edward, Duke of Kent, a major-general, took part in the capture of Martinique and St Lucia in 1794. The youngest brother, Adolphus, Duke of Cambridge, served as a volunteer with the forces in the Low Countries, but later held command positions, and George's nephew, William, Duke of Gloucester, fought with distinction in the Low Countries.

Despite George's support, Addington resigned in April 1804, thus protecting the royal prerogative of choosing ministers rather than being forced out by parliamentary action, which would have left George with fewer options. Pitt, who had turned against Addington, returned to office; but, considering Fox an opponent of necessary measures against France, and as unsound over the position of the Church, George vetoed Pitt's proposal for Fox's inclusion in the government, which, to Pitt, seemed the best way to create a ministry that would survive the reign. This refusal led to deteriorating relations between George and the Prince of Wales, whom the king continued to keep from military service, repeating his own experience at the hands of George II.

After Pitt died in January 1806, George tried to form a new ministry out of the remains of that of Pitt, but he failed and was obliged to turn to the opposition. Indeed, the negotiation that resulted in the 'Ministry of All the Talents', with William, Lord Grenville as prime minister, represented a defeat for George, repeating that of the creation of the Fox-North coalition. Neither were the issues posed by his son's succession lessening. More positively, George also displayed in 1806 an enforced flexibility that he was not to show frequently, not least his regret over the death of Fox in September.

This ministry saw the abolition of the slave trade, which George did not back. He had accepted Sir William Dolben's 1788 bill to lessen crowding on slave ships, but abolition was different, and the king's opposition helped ensure that, like parliamentary reform in 1785, it could not in the 1790s become a ministerial measure that benefited from the weight of government support. For George, however, abolition did not raise comparable concerns to Catholic Emancipation, and he accepted the legislation of 1806–7 that banned the trade. George's sympathies were certainly not engaged by a cause that moved many of his subjects, which, to modern eyes, serves as a stain on his reputation. George, however, was not alone among convinced Christians in defending slavery and the slave trade, and for him issues of property rights and prudence came first, which highlights the degree to which what were viewed as moral issues varied by individual.

The slave trade, like the transportation of convicts and the treatment of Aboriginal peoples, explains why George's reign has an ambiguous memory across parts of the world, and the anniversaries of claims of territory for the king are especially controversial in Australia. The material George retained for his private working library indicates his interest in the transoceanic world. It includes James Cook's original drawings for the survey of St Pierre and Miquelon, islands off Newfoundland, as well as a set of topographical drawings of the new Australian colony. The king financed Cook's first voyage to the Pacific and supported the establishment of botanic gardens at Kew, Calcutta and St Vincent, in order to spread botanical knowledge.

George was happy to approve transportation of felons for life to Botany Bay as a way to build up the new colony in Australia, where a base was first established in 1788. The following year, he was concerned when three convicted felons chose death instead of transportation: 'It is shocking that men can be so lost to every sentiment of gratitude not to feel the mercy shown them in sparing their lives,' a rejection of a royal act. They were cajoled into changing their mind.[4] To George, crime represented a defiance of divine guidance that required admonition. This was a heavy duty, and one that he found increasingly difficult to undertake optimistically; referring in 1802 to those who were to be transported, he wrote: 'as to the reforming the morals of those who have deserved that punishment the King from now a long experience is not sanguine in expectations on that head.'[5] Seriousness, a clear sense of morality and an awareness of duty were all clearly present in George's attitude to his role in confirming death sentences. The king was willing to be merciful, responding favourably to recommendations for mercy, but he could also reject them. He believed in the exemplary nature of punishment and was concerned for due process in the form of maintaining the authority of the judiciary.

George, meanwhile, increasingly focused his life on Windsor, and he moved his effects there from St James's. He last visited Kew in January 1806, never living in the castellated palace he was having built there at great expense, and he last visited Weymouth in 1805. Within the Gothic splendour of Windsor Castle, George dwelled in comfort, his apartments containing thick-pile rugs, Grecian couches and many books. George had spent over £133,000 from his privy purse on building and decoration at Windsor in the then fashionable Gothic style, and his patronage, as well as illustrating his artistic taste and sensibility, helped make Gothic the national style. St George's Chapel was remodelled as part of George's revival of the cult of the Garter, an important aspect of Windsor's role as a setting for exemplary kingship. Benjamin West, who, in 1792, became second President of the Royal Academy, was employed to decorate St George's Hall with eight pictures from the life of Edward III (r. 1327–77) and also to produce a series on the progress of revealed religion.

Relations with the 'Ministry of All the Talents' collapsed

over Catholic Emancipation, which the king's opposition thwarted in March 1807. George's desire to have everything under control, and to banish his own anxiety, then led him to demand a written pledge not to raise the issue anew, and over this the king and his ministers parted company. This made the role of the Crown a contentious issue again and was to loom large in the Whig myth about George. In fact, the Whigs had proposed the change in a way designed to mislead the king, but it had not worked: he was still more a master of government business than many ministers. Trying to mislead George was foolish, and only encouraged his self-righteousness. He had, similarly, avoided being outmanoeuvred in 1783–4.

The next ministry, that headed by the elderly William, 3rd Duke of Portland (1807–9), a conservative Whig and, ironically, the prime minister of the Fox-North coalition who had joined Pitt in the crisis over the French Revolution, was properly mindful that it was the king's ministry. Support for George and 'No Popery' were the issues that dominated the general election held in May–June 1807, and the ministry won a large majority, while its dependence on George was underlined in 1808 when he refused to comply with the ministerial wish that he make known his support for an Offices in Reversion Bill designed to increase Parliament's power and to cut expenditure on sinecures. Without this support, the ministry could not count on the backing of the peers or the bishops, and the bill had to be abandoned. George kept himself informed politically, not least on parliamentary debates, and he intervened during the disputes within the ministry in 1809 centred on the bitter rivalry between George Canning and Robert, Viscount Castlereagh. Whatever the theory of Cabinet cohesion, ministerial divisions left a continued role for the Crown.

George also played a major role in securing the reconstitution of the ministry that October when Spencer Perceval replaced Portland, who was close to death. An able debater and effective minister, who was from a very different social bracket from that of Portland, Perceval had merit, but George wanted him because he trusted him, both as an individual whom he respected and as an Evangelical Protestant who had no truck with Catholic Emancipation. In the negotiations surrounding the formation of the new government George's views had to be heeded, and Perceval had to reassure him that an approach for Whig support would not entail raising the Catholic question, a policy which the Whigs would not accept. As a result of the failure of his approach, when Perceval became First Lord of the Treasury it was as head of a narrowly based ministry that many did not expect to last. In the same way, the Prince Regent's similar attempt to broaden the ministry after the assassination of Perceval in 1812 also failed. More generally, when considering George III's mistakes, it is important to assess the parameters of the possible and to consider comparisons.

Although his eyesight continued very poor, George's health did not otherwise markedly deteriorate in the late 1800s. There were many rumours about him, nevertheless, some opposition MPs claiming in December 1807 that he must be mad because he rarely left Windsor, while in early 1809 a report of his death led to a rise in the price of black cloth. Furthermore, after his attack of mania in February 1804, George's health did not return to its previous equilibrium and he remained easily agitated, leading Pitt that March to avoid meetings likely to upset him. He was unable to attend the spectacular Jubilee fête held in 1809 at Frogmore, only a mile from Windsor. Instead, a portrait of the king was displayed in the temporary temple erected for the occasion. The Jubilee provided a major opportunity for the display of respect and affection for the king as a central part of patriotism; and celebrations were held across the empire, although there were, unsurprisingly, criticisms of the occasion from radicals. In Weymouth, where the Jubilee left a permanent mark in the form of a life-sized statue of George, unveiled in 1810, the mixed popularity of the king was shown in the refusal of some prominent citizens to subscribe to it, but these were years of an apotheosis for George, who became more significant than ever as a symbol of Britain.[6]

George's health permanently broke down towards the close of 1810. As late as 18 October, he was able to write to Charles Yorke, the First Lord of the Admiralty, approving a promotion and adding: 'The King is truly sensible of the affectionate manner in which Mr Yorke has noticed the distress under which His Majesty suffers from the precarious state of his dear daughter.'[7] The shock of the fatal illness of his last-born, his favourite daughter Amelia, proved crucial to George's deterioration. It was initially thought that he would be all right despite her illness, but the fact that she did not die quickly helped cause the crisis, and they both declined together. George frequently questioned her doctors on her progress, and was popularly supposed to have been pushed over the edge when Amelia gave him a mourning ring containing a lock of her hair. Symptoms of insanity were obvious by 25 October, the day of his last public appearance.

The ministry moved quickly. On 10 December 1810, Perceval introduced a Regency Bill, based on Pitt's bill of 1788. The Regency Act passed on 5 February 1811, with royal assent signified by a commission, and George, Prince of Wales was sworn in as regent on 6 February. The act and the resulting oaths emphasized the possibility of recovery and for the first year, at the insistence of Perceval, and against the wishes of the Whigs, the prince's powers were accordingly limited. George's care was entrusted to Charlotte under the Regency Act, but it was a trying responsibility. The deterioration of his condition in July meant that he was physically restrained. Despite the opiates he was given in the form of laudanum, sleep proved difficult, while he ate little and his awareness of the world around him was limited.

In 1812, after the Privy Council had been told by George's doctors on 4 February that their patient was insane, the Prince Regent gained the full prerogative powers of the Crown. He was to follow his father in stressing patriotism, duty and the wish for an inclusive ministry, and not to reward the Whig opposition. On 1 June 1811, Dr Robert Willis took over the total management of George's health, and this change extended to the king's personal circumstances: his pages were replaced by Willis's keepers. George was again exposed to the 1788 system of seclusion and restraint, a policy that, by cutting him off, made him increasingly isolated. Elderly, blind and deaf, George was far less fit than he had been in 1788–9. Kept in his apartments in Windsor, and out of touch with the world, George no longer recognized his family and took solace in imaginary conversations, for example with Lord North. Disconcerted by his state, most of his relatives showed scant interest in him, Princess Augusta preferring to remember him rather than to see him as he now was. Charlotte was in effect a widow. This situation remained largely unchanged for the last years of his life, although on Charlotte's death in 1818, Frederick, Duke of York was appointed guardian. George's declining health left him unaware of the deaths of those close to him. *George III during his Last Illness*, attributed to Joseph Lee, was a portrait of a man far removed from grandeur.

Meanwhile, with clear naval superiority, British sway spread across the world. The range of conquests astonished and awed contemporaries. Cape Town was taken from the Dutch in 1806 and, from the French, Martinique in 1809, and Guadeloupe, Réunion and Mauritius in 1810. Batavia, the centre of Dutch power on Java, fell in 1811, although it was to be restored as part of the peace settlement. In addition, gains were made at the expense of non-European powers: the kingdom of Kandy in Sri Lanka was conquered in 1815, the Gurkhas of Nepal were defeated in 1815–16 and the Marathas in India followed in 1817–18. The absence of triumph in the war of 1812 with America, fought from 1812 to 1815, had far less impact in Britain than the complete crushing of Napoleon at Waterloo in 1815, a key achievement for forces fighting in George's name. Hanover had been liberated in the German War of Liberation in 1813. The defeats of the American War of Independence and the travails of the French Revolutionary Wars had been cast totally into the shadows, and it was not surprising that George's reign would be looked back on as a period of outstanding glory.

The king died in seclusion, if not obscurity, in his room overlooking the North Terrace at Windsor, of pneumonia, on the evening of 29 January 1820, aged eighty-one. Having lain in state for two days, he was buried in St George's Chapel on 16 February, returning to a building on which he had lavished so much attention. As George IV was ill with pleurisy, York was the chief mourner, and large numbers attended the funeral of a man who had seen so much history and who had been the king of the overwhelming majority for their entire lives.

8
An Impressive King

When you're gone, I'll go mad
. . .
I will kill your friends and family to remind you of my love.
  George III in *Hamilton* (2015)

The American presentation of George III, the 'other' against whom they rebelled, is very different from accounts of him appearing from the 1970s in Britain, where the king largely ceased to be kept to the fore as a major focus for criticism in the Whiggish account of progress towards liberty and, instead, passed into the relative obscurity of history. This gave space for a more favourable perception, as was seen in the 1972 biography by John Brooke which contained a foreword by Prince Charles. At the same time, George rather dropped from attention in the 1970s and 1980s. Despite first-rate research by specialists, academic interest in royalty receded in favour of a concern with social topics and popular politics, while public interest in individuals became more democratic. In so far as the English and British royals enjoyed attention, it was the Tudors and, to a lesser extent, the Stuarts who commanded pages and screens. By the early 1990s, George was a largely forgotten figure, other than in the United States.

This situation changed thanks to Alan Bennett, who, in emphasizing a shared humanity, made George a recognizable figure to modern sensibilities. Moreover, positive accessible biographies were produced by Christopher Hibbert (1998) and Christopher Wright (2005), while Prince Charles presented his ancestor as not only sympathetic but impressive, notably in 2004 in both a television interview and in the foreword to the catalogue for the prominent exhibition in the Queen's Gallery of works linked to George from the Royal Collection:

> In the sixty years of his reign he immersed himself in a tremendous range of practical, scientific and artistic interests including agriculture, astronomy, architecture, horology and the collecting of books, medals, paintings and drawings. His absorption with architecture and his skill as an architectural draughtsman I found particularly stimulating and appealing, while his creation of the King's Library and his wish to give encouragement to artists by founding the Royal Academy have been of lasting benefit to the cultural life of this country.[1]

The musical *Hamilton* has reset popular understanding of George in the late 2010s, the king serving as comic relief as well as appearing sinister. However, in 2004 Prince Charles had, in an approach that was to have been restated in 2020 in a major exhibition at Kew Palace, 'George III: The Mind Behind the Myth', better captured part of the quality and range of George's personality and interests, factors that can be crowded out by the emphasis on politics.

These included a strong religious faith, a passion for hunting and an interest in art, architecture, music, astronomy and exploration. That George was faced by major crises in the shape of rebellion in America and Ireland and wars with France was not somehow separate from his attitudes, for the king was stubbornly unwilling to accept both alternative points of view and compromise. Nor were crises limited to his reign: his four predecessors had faced war with France as well as real, or attempted, Jacobite insurrections.

Comparisons with other rulers can extend to American presidents. The first, George Washington, president from 1789 to 1797, was willing to give up power and not seek a presidency for life, which was important to the creation of the particular American combination of elected legitimacy and responsible stability, a solution never seen in Britain. There was to be no military dictatorship in the United States, which was a comment not simply on separate developments there, but also on the shared legacy of British monarchy; a legacy that the Americans, with their collective myth about George, neglected. The key element was not that of the forms and symbols of authority, which of course engage the attention of the camera, but rather that of the goal of rule and the theme of governance. In this respect there was much more similarity between Britain and America than is generally appreciated, for in both the legacy was that of limited government, rule under the law and a sense of accountability, and a contract was the basis for the position of the leader. In America it was that of election in accordance with the constitution; in Britain it was the Glorious Revolution and the subsequent Revolution Settlement.

George was very conscious of his position as a dynastic ruler on terms, a situation that was historic as much as modern, and that consciousness affected his views of his *métier*, of the key issues that faced him, and of his heir. Alongside his interest in Montesquieu and William Blackstone, and his related ability to reflect on the nature and purpose of sovereignty, history lay heavy on George. Just as Washington in 1782–3 rejected the example of Oliver Cromwell in backing the army against Congress, so George was not going to use his control of the army to change the constitution: for example, he was prepared to see troops sent into London in 1780 to suppress the Gordon Riots, but did not try to use them in order to expand royal power. Henry Fox had warned in the early 1760s that factious opposition might lead to continental-style despotism, but George's care for those under him, including his troops, was not intended as a prelude to an increase of his power. After an audience with George in 1787, Sir John Sinclair quoted him on Gustavus III's suppression of the Swedish Age of Liberty in 1772: 'I never will acknowledge that the King of a limited monarchy can on any principle endeavour to change the constitution and increase his own power. No honest man will attempt it.'[2]

This attitude was an important similarity with Washington, and the two men, who were of the same generation, shared a commitment to public virtue based on duty, integrity and steadfastness. George sought to match Washington's self-control and, at the outset of his reign, shared the latter's eventual desire to new-mould the body politic, while the king also retained his conviction that public service was a duty, not a spoils system. As president, Washington, who initially favoured as a title 'His High Mightiness, the President of the United States and Protector of Their Liberties', acted like an elected Patriot King,[3] referring to himself in the third person, accepting royal-style iconography, appearing in state in a highly ornamental coach attended by four servants in livery, establishing very formal levees and going on progresses that were akin to those of monarchs. This helped create a Republican opposition headed by Thomas Jefferson and James Madison that was similar to that of the British Whigs. However, the presidency was not to be for life and, instead, provided a way to manage the transition of power from the Crown.

Outside the English-speaking world, in the absence of its political assumptions and of a benign international context, it was very difficult to sustain an effective limited monarchy. In Poland, the attempt in the early 1790s to create a limited monarchy that owed much to the British model was cut short by Russian invasion, while in France a revolution that began in 1789 as an attempt to centre legitimate limited monarchy on a representative element failed as such. In contrast, the legitimist monarchy of Britain adjusted to crises including the problem posed by the illness and madness of the monarch. Under George, constitutional ambiguity could have developed into constant acrimony, and despite the fears of critics, notably in 1783–4, the king helped create a businesslike monarchy intent on security and upholding the constitution, and not on the accumulation of power and absolute control. Moreover,

George's 'enmity to novelty'[4] accorded with the widespread conservatism of most of British society.

Yet, for a monarch to be in line with wider cultural, social and political currents did not mean that there was no tension, not least because these currents did not command universal support nor preclude both partisan differences and issues of implementation. In contradiction to the Whig and American image of George as a tyrant, or at least a would-be tyrant, he had a strong conviction of the value of limited monarchy and was a willing student of the lessons of the Glorious Revolution and the subsequent Revolution Settlement, and thus a Whig of sorts, albeit one who wanted to bring latter-day Tories into a national consensus.

Yet the criticism he encountered in part reflected his own political mismanagement, while the fixation with the Glorious Revolution has its problems: George saw it as a once-and-for-all settlement that should not be revised, whereas in practice it was a critical stage in a more incremental development of constitutional practice and political culture. Thus, alongside the reaction against the French Revolution, George contributed to a damming-up of political change from the 1780s. Earlier, limited monarchy was to be validated by the notion of the Patriot King, but the 1760s showed the difficulty of the idea, however well intentioned it was. Moreover, an activist monarchy itself faced problems.

Although George had much in common with Elizabeth II, there were significant differences in his role, particularly his far closer commitment to the politics of the situation, as well as his more general position as the working head of a spreading world empire. In common, aside from difficulties with their families, were the strong sense of duty and the piety (as well as the interest in outdoor activities), but George, in addition, began with an intention to reform the British world, and ended as a conservative consolidator of the system and an alternative figure to Napoleon, roles not comparable to the tasks facing Elizabeth II, while George's interest in the arts, literature and the sciences were not matched by her. Instead, Prince Charles is more similar to George in his engagement with the arts and possibly in an activist political interest.

The contrast in political role reflected not developments during George's reign, but those subsequent to it. Instead, in many respects his resetting of the parameters of the British monarchy was more successful than a focus on failure over America might suggest. This resetting in part related to the roles that came to the fore in the modern monarchy, including charitable work and publicly accessible ceremony, which were notable features of George's activity from the late 1780s. There was also the movement from a monarchy defined by the reaction against the Stuarts, both in 1688–9 and later in response to the Jacobite claimants, to one that was consciously intended by Bolingbroke, Frederick and George to serve the nation more inclusively. This practice, let alone goal, proved elusive in the 1760s, but was more on offer from the mid 1780s, and especially from the 1790s in reaction against the growing radicalism of the French Revolution. During the French Revolutionary and Napoleonic Wars (1793–1815), 'Throne and Altar' ideology became stronger, while Toryism was recreated as a politics of patriotism and nationalism. There was also a renewed interest in revealed theology – revelation, providentialism and Biblicism – rather than in apparent natural religious truths.

That resetting was significant because the divisive nature of the monarchy, a division that, in different circumstances, went back to the fifteenth century, had long posed a major political strain which threatened the very stability of the state. Overcoming this entailed an interaction of monarch and circumstances that posed both opportunities and problems for George and his ministers, and, as earlier over America, the margin of success and failure was closer than suggestions of a pattern might indicate. Nevertheless, even if George was sometimes lucky in allies, opponents and circumstances, he was able to take part in a realignment that helped Britain survive the multiple crises of the second half of his reign.

Struggle was a central theme in national identity, and this struggle had a moral character that is difficult to capture today. There was struggle against vice, international and domestic, political and religious, a theme that linked moralists with very different political prospectuses but that also captured the moral obligations of statehood. Liberty and religion seemed to be dependent upon the moral calibre of the people; in a long-standing Tory theme, this calibre was threatened by subversion encouraged, at times, by poor governance and, to a degree, a lack of adequate leadership by the social elite. Furthermore, the achievements of the past that had led to the present situation were no more than stages upon the road, as nationhood had to be defended, not least if the country wished to be assured of the continual support of Providence. This defensiveness accorded with the belief that Anglo-Saxon liberties had been overthrown by the Norman Conquest of 1066. Thus, nationalism was not only identified with divine support but was cumulative, a matter of past as well as present, and of structures as well as events. The Handel celebrations held in 1784–91, strongly supported by George, showed the continuing popularity of the idea of Britain (in practice, England) as an 'elect nation', a second Israel, chosen by God. Toryism, increasingly shorn from the late 1740s of its earlier Jacobitism, was integrated under George into a national political culture and language. In addition, the sense and stability of the locality were building blocks to those of the nation, and those of the nation the guarantee of the situation in the locality. The role of religion was crucial in these equations.

Jane Austen, an Anglican and a Tory, did not deal with the court, of which she had no experience, but her piety, her well-observed and deeply felt understanding of human nature and her nuanced characters provide a way to approach, indeed settle ourselves in, a society that meant much to her contemporary ruler, George, who both reflected and helped stimulate her picture of Englishness and English life. Politics and religion are only in the background in Austen's novels for most modern readers, but each is in fact present. At the party at the Coles' house in *Emma* (1815), 'politics and Mr Elton' were talked over.[5] A sense of Englishness, with a specific mention to that end, was captured in *Persuasion* (1817), and it was no accident that it was presented in the rural light that George relished. Moreover, the reference to the long-established authority of squire and parson captured the joined themes of continuity and legitimacy. Even the change that had occurred was scarcely disruptive:

> Uppercross was a moderate-sized village, which a few years back had been completely in the old English style; containing only two houses superior in appearance to those of the yeomen and labourers, – the mansion of the 'squire, with its high walls, great gates, and old trees, substantial and unmodernised – and the compact, tight parsonage, enclosed in its own neat garden, with a vine and a pear-tree trained round its casements; but upon the marriage of the young 'squire, it had received the improvement of a farmhouse elevated into a cottage for his residence.[6]

Far more than landscape is involved in Englishness, as is made clear in *Northanger Abbey* (1817), in which the sensible Henry Tilney, a clergyman, offers a justified correction to Catherine Morland's suspicion that his father was a murderer:

> What have you been judging from? Remember the country and the age in which we live. Remember that we are English, that we are Christians . . . Does our education prepare us for such atrocities? Do our laws connive at them? Could they be perpetrated without being known, in a country, like this, where social and literary intercourse is on such a footing; where every man is surrounded by a neighbourhood of

voluntary spies, and where roads and newspapers lay every thing open?[7]

Englishness is a theme when Catherine, once rebuked by Henry, comes to appreciate that she has been misled by her reading:

> Charming as were all Mrs Radcliffe's works, and charming even as were the works of all her imitators, it was not in them perhaps that human nature, at least in the midland counties of England, was to be looked for ... there was surely some security for the existence even of a wife not beloved, in the laws of the land, and the manners of the age. Murder was not tolerated, servants were not slaves ... Among the Alps and Pyrenees, perhaps, there were no mixed characters ... But in England it was not so; among the English, she believed, in their hearts and habits, there was a general though unequal mixture of good and bad.[8]

Austen brought this mixture into clear view without probing Catherine's unintentionally amusing suggestion that the situation might be less benign in the further reaches of England. When Abbey Mill Farm is depicted in *Emma* as English and 'seen under a sun bright, without being oppressive',[9] the implied contrast is with the oppression of continental countries, notably, but not only, France. This is a pointed contrast given the long conflict with that country, and also one that underlines the role of war with France in the development and expression of English patriotism and culture.

Earlier, in 1796, Fanny (Frances) Burney, who had been Keeper of the Robes to Charlotte from 1786 to 1790, who remained friendly with the royal family and who was of interest to Austen,[10] presented her novel *Camilla; or, A Picture of Youth* to George and Charlotte. The male characters have faults, but also show an awareness that perfection is not the human condition, a point biographers should heed. Edgar Mandlebert, the wealthy hero, is judgemental, difficult and overly concerned about appearances. Camilla's father, a cleric, is a positive figure, but her older brother, Lionel, is highly mischievous and selfish, and her cousin Clermont is harsh to the servants and a bully. The cleric as a positive figure offers another way to approach George, who was as close as Britain got in modern times to a clerical monarch.

Image played, and continues to play, a key role in the popular understanding of George, but his character and impact were better understood by contemporaries, notably from the 1770s, than in the modern media perspective. Crucially, fortitude was more to the fore in George's achievement and style than stubbornness, for with fortitude came the religious commitment and sense of duty that, to him, monarchy entailed. George was a monarch of dedication and mission affected by the frictions of reality and the pressures of problems, each reflecting the interplay of authority and power. The interactions of personality, purpose and policy were made more difficult by his position as head of his people, not least due to his role in the Church of England as Supreme Governor, and these interactions presented major issues of flexibility in dealing with American and

Irish Patriots, and with Nonconformists. The continuing problems posed by Ireland were one of the most damaging legacies of his reign and left the danger that Ireland was going to be another America. The Irish issue underlines the extent to which the Bolingbrokean concept of 'Patriot King' – which provides insight not only into the king's character but also into a transformation in British political culture that made the king (and for Americans, president) 'above parties' an attractive figure – did not work in all contexts.

Understandably, Whiggish British contemporaries and later commentators, and their American counterparts, are apt to play favourites, assuming that Whigs (and their descendants) or Democrats are on the 'right side of history' and George III was not. However, the king, and notably so after the American war, cultivated the kind of character that many of his subjects admired. And his devotion to the constitution (and, therefore, the established Church) was crucial to his popularity. Moreover, his quasi-Evangelical profile and modest personal habits resonated with what would come to be known as the 'middle class', even as he kept the door shut to Dissenters. George was convinced that the defence of legal authority was a necessity, writing in 1793: 'I most devoutly pray to Heaven that this constitution may remain unimpaired to the latest posterity as a proof of the wisdom of the nation and its knowledge of the superior blessings it enjoys.'[11] His qualities are easier to understand for those who prize commitment, devotion, duty and integrity, than in a modern age when scorn and satire, even hatred of the nation's history, are often prominent. Understanding George and his reign is crucial to our post-progressivist consideration of the history of patriotism (and nationalism), and of how we think about the people or nation, then and now. Far from being an archaic throwback to or relic of the British *ancien régime*, George III was a significant figure who played a key role in shaping the future of 'modern' politics.

Notes

1. AN EARNEST YOUNG MAN

1. Aberystwyth, National Library of Wales, MS 1352 fos 59–60.
2. BL Add. 32684 fo. 78.
3. BL Add. 51439 fos 537–8.
4. George to Bute, 1759, BL Add. 36796 fo. 46.
5. Ibid.
6. Charles Delafaye to Edward Weston, 28 Jan. 1761, Iden Green, Weston-Underwood papers.
7. George to Bute, 14 Dec. 1760, BL Add. 36796 fo. 65.

2. A YOUNG KING

1. George, draft BL Add. 32684 fo. 121.
2. BL Add. 51439 fo. 4.
3. Secker, notes, Lambeth Palace Library, MS 1130/I fos 177, 174.
4. Chesterfield to Richard Chevenix, Bishop of Waterford, 12 Sept. 1761, Blooming-ton, Ind., Lilly Library, Chesterfield papers, Chesterfield-Chevenix correspondence volume.
5. Sir Joshua Reynolds to Lord Grantham, 20 July 1773, Bedford, Bedfordshire County Record Office, Lucas papers 30/14/326/2.
6. Hannecken report, 29 Nov. 1771, Copenhagen, Danske Rigsarkivet, Dept. of Foreign Affairs, vol. 1952.
7. J. Grieg (ed.), *The Diaries of a Duchess: Extracts from the Diaries of the First Duchess of Northumberland* (London: Hodder & Stoughton, 1926), p. 79.
8. Chesterfield to Bute, 9 Apr. 1761, Mount Stuart, Cardiff papers, 6/82.
9. Dreyer, 31 Dec. 1781, 22, 29 Mar., 2, 12 July 1782, 4 July 1783, Danske Rigs-arkivet, vols 1965–6.
10. Elizabeth to Edward Montagu, 23 Nov. 1762, San Marino, Calif., Huntington Library, Montagu papers.
11. Haslang to Baron Wachtendonck, Palatine Foreign Minister, 31 Mar. 1761, Munich, Hauptstaatsarchiv, Bayerischer Gesandtschaft, London, vol. 238.
12. J. Bullion, *Prelude to Disaster: George III and the Origins of the American Revolution, 1751–1763* (New York: Peter Lang, 2017).

3. AN INTERLUDE OF PEACE

1. Sir Joshua Reynolds to Lord Grantham, 20 July 1773, Bedford, Bedfordshire County Record Office, Lucas papers 30/14/362/2.

2. Stanley to Lady Spencer, 29 June 1773, BL Add. 75688.

3. George to North, 5 Oct. 1778, Royal Archives (RA) GEO/3089.

4. I. R. Christie, 'George III and the Debt on Lord North's Election Account, 1780–84', *English Historical Review*, 78 (1963), pp. 715–24.

5. G. W. Rice, 'Archival Subjects for the Life and Career of the Fourth Earl of Rochford', *Archives*, 20 (1992), pp. 265–6; Sinclair to Hawkesbury, 2 July, 22 Sept. 1787, BL Add. 38222 fos 90, 130.

6. George to Grenville, 27 Sept. 1793, BL Add. 58857 fo. 162.

7. M. Guttmacher, *America's Last King: An Interpretation of the Madness of George III* (New York: Scribner's, 1941).

8. T. J. Peters and D. Wilkinson, 'King George III and Porphyria: A Clinical Re-examination of the Historical Evidence', and T. J. Peters and A. Beveridge, 'The Madness of King George III: A Psychiatric Re-assessment', *History of Psychiatry*, 21, 1 (2010), pp. 3–19, 20–37.

9. H. Angelo, *Reminiscences of Henry Angelo* (2 vols, London, 1828–30), vol. 1, p. 354.

10. George to Duke of Gloucester, 9 Nov. 1771, RA GEO/15938.

11. RA GEO/Add. 32.

12. George to William, Lord Grenville, Foreign Secretary, 24 Nov. 1799, BL Add. 58861 fo. 64.

13. George to Earl of Sandwich, 13 Aug. 1773, National Maritime Museum, Sandwich papers, SAN F/45c/16.

14. J. H. Plumb, *New Light on the Tyrant George III* (Lanham, Md.: University Press of America, 1977), pp. 16–17.

4. AMERICAN DEBACLE

1. BL Eg. 982 fo. 12.

2. P. O. Hutchinson (ed.), *The Diary and Letters of His Excellency Thomas Hutchinson* (2 vols, Boston, Mass.: Houghton Mifflin, 1884–6), p. 159.

3. George to North, 11 Sept., 18 Nov. 1774, in J. B. Fortescue (ed.), *The Correspondence of King George the Third* (6 vols, London: Macmillan, 1927–8), vol. 3, pp. 131, 153.

4. John Wesley, *A Concise History of England, from the Earliest Times, to the Death of George II* (4 vols, London: 1776), vol. 3, pp. 107–8.

5. *Parliamentary Register*, III (1775), 42–3.

6. E. Nelson, *The Royalist Revolution: Monarchy and the American Founding* (Cambridge, Mass.: Harvard University Press, 2014).

7. George to Jenkinson, 14 Apr. 1780, BL Loan 72/1 fo. 39.

8. J. Roberts (ed.), *George III and Queen Charlotte: Patronage, Collecting and Court Taste* (London: Royal Collection Publications, 2004); D. Watkin, *The Architect King: George III and the Culture of the Enlightenment* (London: Royal

Collection Publications, 2004); J. Marsden (ed.), *The Wisdom of George the Third* (London: Royal Collections Publications, 2004).

9. George to Jenkinson, 8 June 1780, BL Add. 38564 fo. 17.

10. C. Williams (ed.), *Sophie in London, 1786* (London: Jonathan Cape, 1936), p. 200.

11. George to Pitt, 25 Mar. 1783, PRO 30/8/103 fo. 11.

12. Duchess to Duke of Manchester, 27 May 1783, Huntingdon, Huntingdonshire County Record Office, DDM 21B/6.

13. J. L. Bullion, 'George III on Empire, 1783', *William and Mary Quarterly*, 3rd series, 51 (1994), pp. 305–9.

14. George to Frederick, 29 Dec. 1780, RA GEO/16222.

15. E. Humphris and E. C. Willoughby, *At Cheltenham Spa* (London: Knopf, 1928), p. 65.

16. D'Eon to Parslin, 1 July 1763, Paris, Archives de Ministère des relations extérieures, Correspondance Politique Angleterre, 450 fo. 430.

17. George to Robinson, 27 Oct. 1779, BL Add. 37834 fo. 170.

5. CRISIS OVERCOME

1. George to Pitt, 23 Dec. 1783, PRO. 30/8/103 fo. 15.

2. George to Richard Grenville, 13 Feb. 1784, BL Add. 70957.

3. George, note, 4 April 1784, New York Public Library, Montague collection, vol. 4.

4. George to Richard Grenville, 29 Aug. 1786, BL Add. 70956.

5. *Berrow's Worcester Journal*, 31 July 1788.

6. J. Black, *British Foreign Policy in an Age of Revolutions, 1783–1793* (Cambridge: Cambridge University Press, 1994), p. 199.

7. George to William Grenville, 4 Aug. 1789, BL Add. 58855 fo. 11.

8. F. Bickley (ed.), *The Diaries of Sylvester Douglas, Lord Glenbervie* (2 vols, London: Constable, 1928), vol. 1, p. 358.

9. George to Prince Augustus, 29 Mar. 1787, in A. Aspinall (ed.), *The Later Correspondence of George III, 1783–1810* (5 vols, Cambridge: Cambridge University Press, 1962–70), vol. 1, p. 274.

10. George to Earl Spencer, 17 Dec. 1800, BL Add. 75839.

11. Brand to Wharton, 12 May 1790, Durham University Library, Wharton papers.

12. Adams to Secretary John Jay, 2 June 1785, in C. F. Adams (ed.), *The Works of John Adams* (10 vols, Boston, Mass.: 1853), vol. 8, pp. 255–7; Adams to Thomas Jefferson, 3 June 1785, in L. J. Cappon (ed.), *The Adams-Jefferson Letters: The Complete Correspondence between Thomas Jefferson and Abigail and John Adams* (Chapel Hill, NC: The University of North Carolina Press, 1988), p. 27.

6. IN RESPONSE TO REVOLUTION

1. George to Lord Pelham, Home Secretary, 20 Nov., 2 Dec. 1802, 21 Jan., 21 Feb. (quote) 1803, BL Add. 33115 fos 103, 108, 114, 120.

2. George to William Grenville, 4 May 1792, BL Add. 58856 fo. 156.

3. George to Hawkesbury, 1 May 1801, BL Loan 72/1 fo. 76.

4. George to William Grenville, 24 Nov. 1799, BL Add. 58861 fo. 64.

5. George to Pitt, 28 June 1800, PRO 30/8/104 fo. 287.

7. 'GOOD KING GEORGE'S GLORIOUS DAYS!'

1. Gilbert and Sullivan, *Iolanthe* (1882).
2. Letter to have been displayed, Kew Palace, 2020 exhibition 'George III: The Mind Behind the Myth'.
3. George to Addington, 14 May 1804, Exeter County Record Office, 152 M/1804/OR 38; George to Hawkesbury, 30 Dec. 1804, BL Add. 38190 fo. 8.
4. William Grenville to George, 20 Sept.; George to Grenville, 20, 21, 24, 25 Sept. 1789, BL Add. 58855 fos 19, 23, 27, 29, 31.
5. George to Thomas Pelham, Home Secretary, 7 Mar. 1802, BL Add. 33115 fo. 56.
6. L. J. Colley, 'The Apotheosis of George III: Loyalty, Royalty and the British Nation, 1760–1820', *Past and Present*, 102 (1984), pp. 94–129.
7. George to Yorke, 18 Oct. 1810, BL Add. 45035 fo. 7.

8. AN IMPRESSIVE KING

1. Foreword to Roberts (ed.), *George III and Queen Charlotte*, p. 7.
2. Sinclair to Hawkesbury, 2 July 1787, BL Add. 38222 fo. 91.
3. R. Ketcham, *Presidents above Party: The First American Presidency, 1789–1829* (Chapel Hill, NC: The University of North Carolina Press, 1984), p. 89.
4. George to Melville, 21 May 1804, BL Add. 40100 fo. 302.
5. *Emma*, book 2, ch. 8.
6. *Persuasion*, book 1, ch. 5.
7. *Northanger Abbey*, book 2, ch. 9.
8. Ibid., ch. 10.
9. *Emma*, book 3, ch. 6.
10. J. Harris, *Satire, Celebrity and Politics in Jane Austen* (Lewisburg, Penn.: Bucknell University Press, 2017).
11. George to Pitt, 8 May 1793, PRO 30/8/103 fo. 494.

Selected Further Reading

George III's extensive papers are the obvious start. Under the auspices of the Georgian Papers Programme, the Royal Archives at Windsor are making all of the Georgian papers relating to George III freely available online, including his correspondence, medical papers and essays. The collection also includes the papers of many other members of the royal family and courtiers, as well as papers relating to the household. The papers form three distinct series: his official papers, his private papers and his correspondence with his siblings and children. Making the king immediately accessible to the history-loving public in an entirely new way, all the papers can be accessed as released via the website www.georgianpapers.com, where one can also find the latest news on the project and reports on the extensive programme of research and events associated with it.

There are many collections containing letters from George, notably those of his ministers, with the largest holding being in the British Library. The editions of different sections of the king's correspondence by J. B. Fortescue, Romney Sedgwick and Arthur Aspinall offer much, but far from all, of the material in these holdings. Recent editions of relevant primary sources include Peter Brown and Karl Schweizer (eds), *The Devonshire Diary: William Cavendish, Fourth Duke of Devonshire. Memoranda on State of Affairs 1759–1762* (London: Royal Historical Society, 1982); John Cannon (ed.), *The Letters of Junius* (Oxford: Oxford University Press, 1978); Jonathan Clark (ed.), *The Memoirs and Speeches of James, 2nd Earl Waldegrave, 1742–1763* (Cambridge: Cambridge University Press, 1988); and Derek Jarrett (ed.), *Memoirs of the Reign of King George III by Horace Walpole* (4 vols, New Haven, Conn. and London: Yale

University Press, 1999). An important source that lacks thorough scrutiny is that of diplomatic correspondence, for foreign envoys not only reported on the king but also spoke to him.

Of recent biographies, Jeremy Black's *George III: America's Last King* (New Haven, Conn. and London: Yale University Press, 2006) is the most thorough archival study, while Andrew Roberts's *George III* (London: Allen Lane, 2021) is eagerly awaited. The family are covered by a range of works including J. Shefrin, *Such Constant Affectionate Care: Lady Charlotte Finch, Royal Governess, and the Children of George III* (Los Angeles, Calif.: L: Cotsen Occasional Press, 2003); F. Fraser, *Princesses: The Six Daughters of George III* (London: John Murray, 2004); and C. Orr (ed.), *Queenship in Britain 1660–1837: Royal Patronage, Court Culture and Dynastic Politics* (Manchester: Manchester University Press, 2002). For culture see J. Roberts (ed.), *George III and Queen Charlotte: Patronage, Collecting and Court Taste* (London: Royal Collection Publications, 2004). Politics and religion are well covered in Grayson Ditchfield, *George III: An Essay in Monarchy* (Basingstoke: Palgrave Macmillan, 2002). For an American dimension see Neil York, *The American Revolution, 1760–1790: New Nation as New Empire* (New York: Routledge, 2016). A particular perspective is provided by D. Donald, *The Age of Caricature: Satirical Prints in the Reign of George III* (New Haven, Conn. and London: Yale University Press, 1996).

Picture Credits

1. Jean-Étienne Liotard, George, Prince of Wales, 1754 (Royal Collection Trust © Her Majesty Queen Elizabeth II, 2020/Bridgeman Images)
2. James Gillray, 'Grandpappa in his Glory!!!', 1796 (© Trustees of the British Museum)
3. Thomas Gainsborough, *Queen Charlotte*, 1782 (Metropolitan Museum of Art, New York, Jules Bache Collection, 1949, acc. no. 49.7.55)
4. John Nixon, 'Royal Dipping', 1789 (© Historic Royal Palaces/Claire Collins/Bridgeman Images)
5. Agostino Carlini, bust of George III, 1773 (© Royal Academy of Arts, London/Paul Highnam)
6. James Gillray, 'Wierd-Sisters; ministers of darkness; minions of the moon', 1791 (© Trustees of the British Museum)
7. Richard Newton, 'A Bugaboo!!!', 1792 (© Trustees of the British Museum)
8. James Gillray, 'Temperance enjoying a frugal meal', 1792 (Metropolitan Museum of Art, New York, gift of Adele S. Gollin, 1976, acc. no. 1976.602.28)
9. Anonymous Irish cartoonist, 'A Dreamer', *c*.1800–10 (© Trustees of the British Museum)
10. Matthew Dubourg after James Pollard, 'His Majesty King George III, returning from hunting', *c*.1820 (Royal Collection Trust © Her Majesty Queen Elizabeth II, 2020/Bridgeman Images)
11. The King's Audience Chamber, Windsor Castle, illustration by Charles Wild from William Henry Pyne, *The History of the Royal Residences*, 1819 (© British Library Board, all rights reserved/Bridgeman Images)
12. Nigel Hawthorne as George in *The Madness of George III*, Lyttelton Theatre, London, 1991 (Donald Cooper/Rex/Shutterstock)
13. Jonathan Groff as George in *Hamilton*, Richard Rodgers Theatre, New York, 2015 (Joan Marcus)
14. Joseph Lee, *George III during his Last Illness*, 1827, after a sketch made by Matthew Wyatt, 1820 (Royal Collection Trust © Her Majesty Queen Elizabeth II, 2020/Bridgeman Images)

Index

Penguin Monarchs

THE HOUSES OF WESSEX AND DENMARK

Athelstan	Tom Holland
Aethelred the Unready	Richard Abels
Cnut	Ryan Lavelle
Edward the Confessor	David Woodman

THE HOUSES OF NORMANDY, BLOIS AND ANJOU

William I	Marc Morris
William II	John Gillingham
Henry I	Edmund King
Stephen	Carl Watkins
Henry II	Richard Barber
Richard I	Thomas Asbridge
John	Nicholas Vincent

THE HOUSE OF PLANTAGENET

Henry III	Stephen Church
Edward I	Andy King
Edward II	Christopher Given-Wilson
Edward III	Jonathan Sumption
Richard II	Laura Ashe

THE HOUSES OF LANCASTER AND YORK

Henry IV*	Catherine Nall
Henry V	Anne Curry
Henry VI	James Ross
Edward IV	A. J. Pollard
Edward V*	Thomas Penn
Richard III	Rosemary Horrox

* Forthcoming

THE HOUSE OF TUDOR

Henry VII*	Sean Cunningham
Henry VIII	John Guy
Edward VI	Stephen Alford
Mary I	John Edwards
Elizabeth I	Helen Castor

THE HOUSE OF STUART

James I	Thomas Cogswell
Charles I	Mark Kishlansky
[Cromwell	David Horspool]
Charles II	Clare Jackson
James II	David Womersley
William III & Mary II	Jonathan Keates
Anne*	Richard Hewlings

THE HOUSE OF HANOVER

George I	Tim Blanning
George II	Norman Davies
George III	Jeremy Black
George IV	Stella Tillyard
William IV	Roger Knight
Victoria	Jane Ridley

THE HOUSES OF SAXE-COBURG & GOTHA AND WINDSOR

Edward VII	Richard Davenport-Hines
George V	David Cannadine
Edward VIII	Piers Brendon
George VI	Philip Ziegler
Elizabeth II	Douglas Hurd

* Forthcoming

ALLEN LANE
an imprint of
PENGUIN BOOKS

Also Published

Stephen Kotkin, *Stalin, Vol. II: Waiting for Hitler, 1928-1941*

Lindsey Fitzharris, *The Butchering Art: Joseph Lister's Quest to Transform the Grisly World of Victorian Medicine*

Serhii Plokhy, *Lost Kingdom: A History of Russian Nationalism from Ivan the Great to Vladimir Putin*

Mark Mazower, *What You Did Not Tell: A Russian Past and the Journey Home*

Lawrence Freedman, *The Future of War: A History*

Niall Ferguson, *The Square and the Tower: Networks, Hierarchies and the Struggle for Global Power*

Matthew Walker, *Why We Sleep: The New Science of Sleep and Dreams*

Edward O. Wilson, *The Origins of Creativity*

John Bradshaw, *The Animals Among Us: The New Science of Anthropology*

David Cannadine, *Victorious Century: The United Kingdom, 1800-1906*

Leonard Susskind and Art Friedman, *Special Relativity and Classical Field Theory*

Maria Alyokhina, *Riot Days*

Oona A. Hathaway and Scott J. Shapiro, *The Internationalists: And Their Plan to Outlaw War*

Chris Renwick, *Bread for All: The Origins of the Welfare State*

Anne Applebaum, *Red Famine: Stalin's War on Ukraine*

Richard McGregor, *Asia's Reckoning: The Struggle for Global Dominance*

Chris Kraus, *After Kathy Acker: A Biography*

Clair Wills, *Lovers and Strangers: An Immigrant History of Post-War Britain*

Odd Arne Westad, *The Cold War: A World History*

Max Tegmark, *Life 3.0: Being Human in the Age of Artificial Intelligence*

Jonathan Losos, *Improbable Destinies: How Predictable is Evolution?*

Chris D. Thomas, *Inheritors of the Earth: How Nature Is Thriving in an Age of Extinction*

Chris Patten, *First Confession: A Sort of Memoir*

James Delbourgo, *Collecting the World: The Life and Curiosity of Hans Sloane*

Naomi Klein, *No Is Not Enough: Defeating the New Shock Politics*

Ulrich Raulff, *Farewell to the Horse: The Final Century of Our Relationship*

Slavoj Žižek, *The Courage of Hopelessness: Chronicles of a Year of Acting Dangerously*

Patricia Lockwood, *Priestdaddy: A Memoir*

Ian Johnson, *The Souls of China: The Return of Religion After Mao*

Stephen Alford, *London's Triumph: Merchant Adventurers and the Tudor City*

Hugo Mercier and Dan Sperber, *The Enigma of Reason: A New Theory of Human Understanding*

Stuart Hall, *Familiar Stranger: A Life Between Two Islands*

Allen Ginsberg, *The Best Minds of My Generation: A Literary History of the Beats*

Sayeeda Warsi, *The Enemy Within: A Tale of Muslim Britain*

Alexander Betts and Paul Collier, *Refuge: Transforming a Broken Refugee System*

Robert Bickers, *Out of China: How the Chinese Ended the Era of Western Domination*

Erica Benner, *Be Like the Fox: Machiavelli's Lifelong Quest for Freedom*

William D. Cohan, *Why Wall Street Matters*

David Horspool, *Oliver Cromwell: The Protector*

Daniel C. Dennett, *From Bacteria to Bach and Back: The Evolution of Minds*

Derek Thompson, *Hit Makers: How Things Become Popular*

Harriet Harman, *A Woman's Work*

Wendell Berry, *The World-Ending Fire: The Essential Wendell Berry*

Daniel Levin, *Nothing but a Circus: Misadventures among the Powerful*

Stephen Church, *Henry III: A Simple and God-Fearing King*

Pankaj Mishra, *Age of Anger: A History of the Present*

Graeme Wood, *The Way of the Strangers: Encounters with the Islamic State*

Michael Lewis, *The Undoing Project: A Friendship that Changed the World*

John Romer, *A History of Ancient Egypt, Volume 2: From the Great Pyramid to the Fall of the Middle Kingdom*

Andy King, *Edward I: A New King Arthur?*

Thomas L. Friedman, *Thank You for Being Late: An Optimist's Guide to Thriving in the Age of Accelerations*

John Edwards, *Mary I: The Daughter of Time*

Grayson Perry, *The Descent of Man*

Deyan Sudjic, *The Language of Cities*

Norman Ohler, *Blitzed: Drugs in Nazi Germany*

Carlo Rovelli, *Reality Is Not What It Seems: The Journey to Quantum Gravity*

Catherine Merridale, *Lenin on the Train*

Susan Greenfield, *A Day in the Life of the Brain: The Neuroscience of Consciousness from Dawn Till Dusk*

Christopher Given-Wilson, *Edward II: The Terrors of Kingship*

Emma Jane Kirby, *The Optician of Lampedusa*

Minoo Dinshaw, *Outlandish Knight: The Byzantine Life of Steven Runciman*

Candice Millard, *Hero of the Empire: The Making of Winston Churchill*

Christopher de Hamel, *Meetings with Remarkable Manuscripts*

Brian Cox and Jeff Forshaw, *Universal: A Guide to the Cosmos*

Ryan Avent, *The Wealth of Humans: Work and Its Absence in the Twenty-first Century*

Jodie Archer and Matthew L. Jockers, *The Bestseller Code*

Cathy O'Neil, *Weapons of Math Destruction: How Big Data Increases Inequality and Threatens Democracy*

Peter Wadhams, *A Farewell to Ice: A Report from the Arctic*

Richard J. Evans, *The Pursuit of Power: Europe, 1815-1914*

Anthony Gottlieb, *The Dream of Enlightenment: The Rise of Modern Philosophy*

Marc Morris, *William I: England's Conqueror*

Gareth Stedman Jones, *Karl Marx: Greatness and Illusion*

J.C.H. King, *Blood and Land: The Story of Native North America*

Robert Gerwarth, *The Vanquished: Why the First World War Failed to End, 1917-1923*

Joseph Stiglitz, *The Euro: And Its Threat to Europe*

John Bradshaw and Sarah Ellis, *The Trainable Cat: How to Make Life Happier for You and Your Cat*

A J Pollard, *Edward IV: The Summer King*

Erri de Luca, *The Day Before Happiness*

Diarmaid MacCulloch, *All Things Made New: Writings on the Reformation*

Daniel Beer, *The House of the Dead: Siberian Exile Under the Tsars*

Tom Holland, *Athelstan: The Making of England*

Christopher Goscha, *The Penguin History of Modern Vietnam*

Mark Singer, *Trump and Me*

Roger Scruton, *The Ring of Truth: The Wisdom of Wagner's Ring of the Nibelung*

Ruchir Sharma, *The Rise and Fall of Nations: Ten Rules of Change in the Post-Crisis World*

Jonathan Sumption, *Edward III: A Heroic Failure*

Daniel Todman, *Britain's War: Into Battle, 1937-1941*

Dacher Keltner, *The Power Paradox: How We Gain and Lose Influence*

Tom Gash, *Criminal: The Truth About Why People Do Bad Things*

Brendan Simms, *Britain's Europe: A Thousand Years of Conflict and Cooperation*

Slavoj Žižek, *Against the Double Blackmail: Refugees, Terror, and Other Troubles with the Neighbours*

Lynsey Hanley, *Respectable: The Experience of Class*

Piers Brendon, *Edward VIII: The Uncrowned King*

Matthew Desmond, *Evicted: Poverty and Profit in the American City*

T.M. Devine, *Independence or Union: Scotland's Past and Scotland's Present*

Seamus Murphy, *The Republic*

Jerry Brotton, *This Orient Isle: Elizabethan England and the Islamic World*

Srinath Raghavan, *India's War: The Making of Modern South Asia, 1939-1945*

Clare Jackson, *Charles II: The Star King*

Nandan Nilekani and Viral Shah, *Rebooting India: Realizing a Billion Aspirations*

Sunil Khilnani, *Incarnations: India in 50 Lives*

Helen Pearson, *The Life Project: The Extraordinary Story of Our Ordinary Lives*

Ben Ratliff, *Every Song Ever: Twenty Ways to Listen to Music Now*

Richard Davenport-Hines, *Edward VII: The Cosmopolitan King*

Peter H. Wilson, *The Holy Roman Empire: A Thousand Years of Europe's History*

Todd Rose, *The End of Average: How to Succeed in a World that Values Sameness*

Frank Trentmann, *Empire of Things: How We Became a World of Consumers, from the Fifteenth Century to the Twenty-First*

Laura Ashe, *Richard II: A Brittle Glory*

John Donvan and Caren Zucker, *In a Different Key: The Story of Autism*

Jack Shenker, *The Egyptians: A Radical Story*

Tim Judah, *In Wartime: Stories from Ukraine*

Serhii Plokhy, *The Gates of Europe: A History of Ukraine*

Robin Lane Fox, *Augustine: Conversions and Confessions*

Peter Hennessy and James Jinks, *The Silent Deep: The Royal Navy Submarine Service Since 1945*

Sean McMeekin, *The Ottoman Endgame: War, Revolution and the Making of the Modern Middle East, 1908–1923*

Charles Moore, *Margaret Thatcher: The Authorized Biography, Volume Two: Everything She Wants*

Dominic Sandbrook, *The Great British Dream Factory: The Strange History of Our National Imagination*

Larissa MacFarquhar, *Strangers Drowning: Voyages to the Brink of Moral Extremity*

Niall Ferguson, *Kissinger: 1923-1968: The Idealist*

Carlo Rovelli, *Seven Brief Lessons on Physics*

Tim Blanning, *Frederick the Great: King of Prussia*

Ian Kershaw, *To Hell and Back: Europe, 1914–1949*

Pedro Domingos, *The Master Algorithm: How the Quest for the Ultimate Learning Machine Will Remake Our World*

David Wootton, *The Invention of Science: A New History of the Scientific Revolution*